The Power of StillPoint

CATHY WILSON

The Power of StillPoint

ISBN 13: 978-0-9822722-7-5

ISBN: 0-9822722-7-8

Library of Congress Control Number: 2009924283

Cover design by All Things That Matter Press

Cover photo by: Dani Simmonds

Published in 2009 by All Things That Matter Press

Printed in the United States of America

Introduction

After running my own editing and ghostwriting business for nearly two decades, an on-again, off-again, solitary proposition, I decided I wanted to change jobs: something more stable and much more sociable. Teaching college was what I really wanted, but with a small town college English department, you can wait a very long time for a position to open up. Teaching part-time—at least in our tightfisted state school economy—brought in very little pay, hardly worth the effort. So every day I scanned the want ads for a position opening, and every day, nothing showed up.

The new semester started and still I read the ads. I think my husband—himself a longtime college professor—felt a little sorry for me, because by the time the school year is underway, you can hardly hope for a new opening to pop up. Then around October I noticed an ad for a position at the college—starting a new program for adult students wishing to get back into school. It was a flexible program to help older students do coursework without attending conventional classes.

I applied and got the job. I loved it! It was so empowering to help adults learn; they were focused and positive and responsive. The job had some drawbacks: I had to travel sixty miles twice a week to teach at a satellite campus, and the administration had designed more hours into the position than most professors teach. During those hours, I reasoned, if no students came in, I could use the time to write—still a plus.

We called the program JumpStart, and it grew fast. We had many adults enroll in the two years we ran it. Then came 9/11, and along with the rest of the nation, our state economy crashed. Our local college budget was suffering some severe problems in addition to huge state budget cuts, and the administration elected to cut any programs they considered extraneous to their core offerings. That meant JumpStart. I could hardly believe it; the success of the program should speak for itself! Our enrollment had grown 600% in just a year! At least half our students had only worked partway through the curriculum. Besides all that, this was my job!

No matter—they cut the program. At first, I crashed and settled into a murky misery, and then, unexpectedly—peace. I felt flooded with stillness, quietness, absolute sureness that everything was just as it should be, and my husband experienced the same thing. *How* that could be we didn't understand, but we were willing to accept it. I applied for unemployment and spent the summer—which would have been filled with JumpStart teaching—gardening, being with the family, and just living.

In order to receive unemployment, you have to make a couple of calls a week and attend some interviews for possible jobs. I went along with this, including an interview to teach high school students at a local detention center—in other words, the local kid jail. At the interview, seven or eight employees, including the program director, sat circled the room and asked me questions. I answered them, but instead of worrying about the interview outcome, I mostly just felt love and appreciation for these people who would devote their lives to kids who really needed help. I came out of the interview happy and filled with love.

As with the other calls and interviews, I didn't hear anything more about this and just continued on with unemployment. I figured I'd do some writing and then go back to freelancing. Then one day, the college called and offered me a temporary position. That same day, the director of the detention center called and offered me a teaching position. Well—I'd much rather teach college; that was for sure. But I went to meet at the detention center, and absolutely fell in love with the facility and the kids. Most importantly, I felt perfect peace, so half an hour after that final interview, I called the director and accepted the job.

It turned out to be one of my life's peak experiences. I didn't have to do any of the things I hated about public school: extended hours, discipline, record-keeping, grade-giving. The staff took care of all of that, and I could just teach. I had no idea such a positive environment even existed in our tiny little town, and from my point of view, I could not have imagined myself in such a job. Everything led up to it in a natural way, although I couldn't have known it before. However, the knowledge *was* there and available—through StillPoint. StillPoint told us that everything was all right and just as it should be, and that gave us the confidence to let go of our stresses and to be at peace.

This is a book about StillPoint: how to do it, how to recognize it, how to use it. StillPoint is a fairly universal experience, although people come to it in many different ways.

Chapter One, StillPoint, Spirit and Body, will let you know what it is and how people use it in spiritual practice. In that chapter you'll also learn what's happening in your body when you experience StillPoint, and how it fits in with other health-care modalities.

Chapter Two, Finding Your StillPoint, will get you started right away in trying it out for yourself. You'll find plenty of examples and exercises to help you begin, including some preparatory exercises, simple and powerful experiences that you can enjoy the rest of your life. Then you'll learn a couple of ways to find your own StillPoint; try them out to see what works for you.

Chapter Three, StillPoint When You Get Sick, gives you some immediate ways to experiment with StillPoint for yourself and your family. Often when we come down with a cold or wake up with a headache, we just reach for the Tylenol® and keep on going. This chapter will take us a step beyond that into understanding our illnesses a little better and finding the best ways to get through them.

Body-mind practitioners are always saying that we don't get sick in a vacuum. Any time we suffer with an ailment, especially over a long period of time, there's bound to be something going on emotionally and spiritually that links up with our condition. **Chapter Four, StillPoint and Chronic Illness,** walks you through understanding chronic illness using StillPoint. Although we're not to blame for our conditions, StillPoint can help us find some of the patterns that might be keeping us down, and it can help us take that first step, then the next, to getting better. As you'll see from reading the stories in this chapter, even long, difficult conditions can improve when we find the way through StillPoint.

Chapter Five, StillPoint and Your Relationships, may bring you peace and understanding in the most difficult areas of all: getting along with our partners, our families, our friends. One of my longtime friends, going through a wrenching divorce, said, "You know, we were soul mates; he was the love of my heart. Yet we couldn't get along; we couldn't make it work." You can use StillPoint to find the essence of what's really going on inside you, and that can help you deal more honestly and lovingly with the ones you care for the most. And if you are raising children, you will find StillPoint an invaluable way to know what to do for them—and how they're doing when they're not home.

If the next chapter, **Everyday StillPoint,** were the only one you read in this book it would still be worth the price of admission. What can you do when you misplace your keys or your address book? How can you know what coursework to take, what route to drive on your trip? This chapter helps you get past the panic and into peace using StillPoint.

In **Chapter Seven, StillPoint and Healing the Past,** we remember the obvious: none of us grew up in a perfect family and all of us have issues we'd like to overcome, hurt feelings we'd like to heal, negative emotions we'd like to be done with. Just knowing that this is part of the universal human condition can be some comfort, but that doesn't necessarily get us through our distress. StillPoint can help, however, allowing us a fresh look at our pain through the lens of peace and more perfect understanding. Stories and exercises help you to peace and healing the traumas of the past.

It's not fortune-telling or psychic divination; it's just **StillPoint and Finding Your Future, Chapter 8.** Wouldn't it be a relief to have a way to measure your life-changing decisions: what job to take, what college to attend, who to hire, what book to read next? StillPoint won't compel you to make a certain choice, but it can help you find the shortest route to your ultimate destiny. And when you come to that crucial crossroads and have to make a decision right *now,* knowing how to find StillPoint can be a lifesaver, saving you time and grief and maybe even saving your life.

We hear it so often that sometimes we lose the importance the meaning: we *are* all connected in this world, and what we do affects others, sometimes in profound and life-changing ways. As you practice StillPoint, you open your heart and grow in compassion and generosity. **Chapter 9, StillPoint and Healing the World,** will help you see how powerful your influence can actually be.

StillPoint is not a passing concept that you might try for a while and move on to some other fad. Instead, it can serve you throughout your life. Once you learn StillPoint, you're in for an adventure, because it will help you pierce through everyday confusion into compassionate, clear sight. I like to say that once you know StillPoint, you'll never be bored, because you'll know and understand stuff you had no idea of before. A nice side benefit: your health will probably improve all the time, and so will your mood. Whatever the question, StillPoint can lead you to the answer, and if it's not what you thought it was going to be, then comes the fun!

Table of Contents

Chapter One: StillPoint, Spirit and Body

What is StillPoint?

StillPoint is a simple body/mind practice that creates a moment of perfect stillness in the body and in the soul. In that moment, we can rest and heal from any troubles we might have, whether physical, emotional, mental, or spiritual.

StillPoint: the words may sound unfamiliar, but the concept is very old and crosses cultures across the world. It's the center of Zen Buddhist practice, fundamental to Christian experience, and close to the Jewish heart. Spiritual seekers have pursued StillPoint for thousands of years, sometimes over whole lifetimes.

You can experience many levels of StillPoint, increasing and ascending till you attain almost perfect stillness. At the same time, most people can learn how to do it—and benefit from it—right away. After that, StillPoint will be a constant delight and source of healing as you reach further and deeper into it. It's not one of those throwaway techniques that you get tired of as soon as you learn it and never use again. StillPoint will serve you all your life, and you'll get better and better at it as you go along. As you practice StillPoint, you may learn to reach stillness anytime, and perhaps most of the time, thereby becoming a healer simply with your presence. Like Gandhi, you will *be* the change you wish to see in the world.

Then again, meditators and others who attain near-perfect stillness will assure you that it's *not* falling asleep or becoming unconscious. If you were to somehow find a point of *absolute* silence and stillness, you would probably go unconscious and your brain would not even be functioning. That's not StillPoint, because StillPoint enhances consciousness and brings you closer and more alive to your inner reality, your inner truth.

In a physical sense, you can know you're in StillPoint by noticing what's going on in your body. Your breathing slows, your heartbeat slows down, your muscles relax throughout your body and, mostly importantly, the CranioSacral rhythm, the cadenced pulsing of your cranial fluid in your cranium and through your spinal column, pauses for a bit. You experience StillPoint as a great physical relief, relaxation, and release. You feel refreshed, renewed, refocused and ready to take on the world.

How does this happen? Using the techniques you'll learn in the next chapter, you'll find you can actually induce StillPoint physically, a fast and effective relaxation practice you can do anytime. You will learn just as easily to find your rhythm and StillPoint without physical aids, and that's where the adventure starts, because it gives you an instant and absolutely reliable bridge between the physical world and the spiritual.

Our physical world is an interesting business. Often meditators say the physical world is a distraction, and it can be, because it gives you false or incomplete messages about what's real, especially when you're dealing with people. The physical world usually hands you incomplete or downright false messages about your worth and what's really at the root of your joy or discontent.

On the other hand, the physical world contains a flow of reality and truth that connects, binds and bonds us to our ultimate reality. The trees, the ocean, the stones, the soil, the plants all speak the truth. They can *only* speak the truth, so when we connect with these things, flowing with them, being of one mind with them, we realize what's real and can connect up to the truth of things. After all, we are physical beings and we live in a physical world, and that world can help keep us true, if we are willing.

Still, the only measure we have for knowing anything is our inner truth, our spiritual knowing of things, and that's what is so fascinating about StillPoint, because it gives us perfect access to what's really going on inside ourselves. You can spend a great deal of time (and money) in talk therapy, in group process work, and similar approaches, and they might do some good yet still miss the essential element, the *one* thing that will begin release you from your pain or open the door to the right direction. StillPoint is the doorway, the opening, the unerring measure of that ultimate truth, because in StillPoint our bodies give us absolute contact with it, and it's never wrong! Once we figure out what's true, we can still choose various ways to deal with it, but if we try to twist the truth or make it mean what it really doesn't, our bodies simply go out of StillPoint and let us know that we need to get back on track. The experience is pleasant, painless and guilt-free. As a matter of fact, it sets us free.

The natural world is ineffably and permanently connected up with the spiritual world. There are lots of ways to talk about the spiritual world, which can be confusing, especially since most of us want to separate the physical world from the spiritual. However, the spiritual world flows throughout the natural world and informs it and gives it life and substance. Every living thing is enlivened by spirit—and many people say that the nonliving things, the rocks and the earth, also have spirit as well.

If you have ever taken care of animals and had pets, you know this is true. Living things can be our teachers and healers because they *know* spiritual things without having the confusing element of language thrown in. For example, one of my friends owns a sweet golden retriever, Pallie. Normally she is a bounding, buoyant dog, but one day she remained lying quietly in the corner of the kitchen, to the point that my friend wondered if there might be something wrong with her. Then her five-year-old daughter Kari came into the kitchen and lay down with the dog. Kari had been coming down with flu and a fever, but she'd been bouncing off the walls, unable to settle down in bed and start to get better. Pallie "knew" that Kari had a need, and she lay still till Kari joined her cuddling in the corner. Within moments, the two were breathing quietly together and Kari fell asleep. Her mom was able to gently lift her and carry her to bed, where she began her recovery. And sure enough, as soon as Kari was safe and sound in bed, Pallie was up bouncing around again, begging for a rousing run through the neighborhood.

In the moment of StillPoint, we can know for certain anything that we want—or need—to know. In many cases, StillPoint can answer questions that we have been struggling with, questions profound or trivial, life changing or just plain helpful. Sam had been struggling with sharp stomach pains that seemed to come and go without any particular pattern. For years he had consulted doctors who had run many tests, but nobody ever came up with an answer for him. The one day, in the shower, he felt himself go into StillPoint and the thought clearly flashed through his mind, "I have diverticulitis." He stood there under the warm water with that thought running through his head, "Diverticulitis.. .hmmmm. . . What's diverticulitis?" He didn't know *what* it was, but his body remained in StillPoint when he retained that thought. So during the next few days, he did some research on the condition and found that his symptoms were indeed exactly those of the ailment. With a little Internet research and some help from an herbalist friend, Sam initiated some life changes, including stress reduction, nutrition, and herbal remedies, that cleared up his condition. He hasn't suffered from it since. His spirit *and* his body worked together to reveal to Sam the truth about his ailment, and he took it from there. Although he didn't run into any hitches figuring out an approach to help himself, if he had needed assistance in finding his way to health, he could have accessed StillPoint to do it.

Even though StillPoint may reveal a truth to us, the gentle nature of this approach does not force or compel us to make any life changes, and indeed leaves us completely free and *guilt-free* in dealing with what we learn. For example, Sharon was trying to figure out why her back hurt her so badly. Sometimes it didn't hurt at all, but occasionally the pain was almost debilitating. So far she hadn't been able to associate her pain with any particular situation or issue, till one day, sitting in her mother's kitchen, she felt herself go into StillPoint with the thought, "You're mad at your mother."

"No, I'm not!" Sharon argued with herself. At that moment, she could feel herself leaving StillPoint, so she "tried on" the new idea once more. "Maybe I'm mad at my mom," she thought, and again felt herself slide peacefully into StillPoint. She didn't pursue the thought any more that day, or even for several weeks, even months. Finally the time came when professional help and personal circumstances came together just right, and Sharon was able to work through her anger and come to some peace with her feelings about her mother. Not surprisingly, from that day forward, her back pain became less and less bothersome, till she often had periods of time when she was pretty much pain free.

In short, learning something new in StillPoint may not require or force you to make any changes right then, although it is always an invitation to do so, because my experience has taught me that your body/spirit will not reveal any truth to you unless you're more or less ready to do something about it.

In a physical sense, nobody knows for *sure* how StillPoint works, although a few interesting and workable models can help us understand it. Perhaps the most common comes from Dr. John Upledger, an osteopath who over many years has pioneered new pathways to healing in CranioSacral© Therapy and similar bodywork practices. Dr. Upledger began his understanding of the CranioSacral rhythm when, as a young medical practitioner, he was asked to assist in a back surgery. The surgeon requested that Dr. Upledger stabilize the dural tube, which is the thick tube encasing the spinal cord and containing the cerebro-spinal fluid, while he performed the surgery. Dr. Upledger found it was nearly impossible to hold the patient's dural tube still; it kept moving and pulsing at seemingly regular intervals. From this he hypothesized that the cerebro-spinal fluid is an enclosed system similar to a hydraulic system. The fluid is consistently refreshed in systemic pulses from a valve located in the brain. These pulses occur about six to twelve times a minute, independent from any other body system though autonomic like the heartbeat or respiration. However, there is an important difference between the CranioSacral rhythm and the other body rhythms. Therapeutic pressures gently applied to the cranial base can influence the CranioSacral rhythm, and it also seems to be affected by our emotional/spiritual state. Over decades of research and clinical application, Dr. Upledger has confirmed again and again that his original hypotheses hold true. He originated a training system that has allowed practitioners all over the world to learn to discern and utilize the subtle rhythm of the CranioSacral system. Of course, surgical research cannot "prove" this system, because any time the dural tube is breached by surgery, the hydraulic system won't work.

Hand in hand with this theory goes the ancient concept of the meridian system, based on Chinese medical theory, which says that our bodies contain a complex and delicate pattern of energy that runs in vertical paths from head to toe. When a person is healthy, the flow of energy along these paths moves along uninterrupted, but when something goes wrong, whether illness, accident, or inherited condition, then the flow is interrupted. Along this pattern are points, called acupuncture or acupressure points, which can access the problem areas and help restore proper flow. For many years, meridian theory was considered to be in the "fringe," but in 1981, researchers attempted an interesting experiment. They injected radioactive isotopes at some of the classical acupuncture points and then tracked the progress of the radioactive material, which traced itself along the body exactly along the meridian lines, although somewhat slowly and sometimes in fits and starts. This gave literal physical testimony to the theretofore-theoretical meridian theory. When a person is suffering from a physical ailment, a practitioner can touch various acupuncture points to determine where the problem might lie, and the body may go into StillPoint to confirm them.

About Knowing

At first blush, most of us believe in the textbook way of understanding things: you read books or learn stuff in other ways, and then you know it. In other words, you have to use your intellect to acquire knowledge and that's how you retain it, too. We have grown up believing that once you learn something, you always know it, even if you may forget it momentarily.

However, most of us have *also* experienced another way of knowing things. Even though we may not have heard something before, we just *know* it. Even though we've never met a person before, we just have a gut feeling that he'll be our friend, or that she is not a safe person. Although we may insist we don't have much intuition, most of us really do.

Sometimes our intuitive knowing becomes stronger in a particular field while remaining undeveloped in others. For example, a law enforcement officer, Jay, has an uncanny sense of when a person is telling the truth. He seems to be able to smell a crook, or a crooked situation, a mile away. When he broke up a methamphetamine lab the other day, we asked him how he found it.

"Well, I stopped this guy for speeding," he said, smiling at the pun. "And something just didn't seem right. He didn't act drunk or anything, but my gut told me that there was something fishy going on. So I tailed him—at a distance—and he drove right up to a house we've been surveilling for a long time. You could definitely smell the acetone in the air. Soon as he saw me pull up, he gunned his engine and sped away. When I finally got him pulled over, I searched his car and sure enough, there was a stash of the drug plus a lot of money. That gave me enough to get a warrant to search the house, and there we found the lab."

What *is* this gut feeling? We can call it intuition, but where does it come from? How do we *know* things we can't logically know? The answer to this is a big key to understanding how StillPoint works.

When things are happening in the physical world, the tangible world around us, they are also impacting the spiritual world, or the world of energy or intangibles that surrounds us. The spiritual world shapes much of what's going on around us physically, whether we're aware of it or not. When an inspirational speaker tells you that what you feel and think will manifest in your outward life, that "as a man thinketh, so is he," you're hearing the same thing. We live in a physical world at present; we're mortals on a physical earth, and that's a good thing, a great source of joy and pleasure. There's not much good in renouncing this physical world for a better one; it's a joy to live right here and now. At the same time, however, we can know that there are spiritual—or if you prefer, energy—realities that influence and shape what's going on around us.

The living things around us, including the plants and animals, are usually tuned to the spiritual realm that affects the physical one. I think that's why shamans often choose a spirit animal, using it to find a path to the spiritual realm. I also think that's why we get our minds clear and priorities straight when we go outside for a walk. The information that we need, perfectly understandable and harmonious, is always there. We just need to step outside our busy thoughts to access it.

StillPoint is a great way to do this, because our own spirits and minds have complete access to the spiritual world around us.

"We are all one," say spiritual practitioners. I believe this is a very literal thing; we all possess a spirit, and that part of us is connected to all of the rest of the spirit around us. It is easy to see that the spirit around us really knows everything—past, present and future. It's no mystery; it's just there. This is a great way to learn just about anything you want to know. Sometimes it's easy to access the information, though, and sometimes it's hard. I believe that if there's something we ought to know, that we can access it easily enough. StillPoint is a simple and direct way to do it. When everything feels right, you can call it "flow." When there's something disruptive or out of balance, you could call it "block." Perfect health is all flow and no blocks, but just about everybody has some blocks and some flow.

So, in the case of Jay the law enforcement officer, he developed the habit of attuning himself to the blocks in the flow relating to lawbreaking, and he has become very good at it. Feeling your body's rhythm and StillPoint is the most direct and simple way I've ever found to discern block and flow. It almost doesn't matter what you want to know; you can find it through StillPoint.

Block and Flow

Here's a little more on block and flow. Back to meridian theory: when energy is flowing nicely throughout our bodies and spirits along the meridians, we are in *flow*. Even though we might have some disorder in our body and even if circumstances around us aren't working well, we are still in balance, feeling good, able to deal with whatever comes along.

In today's' world, most of us don't usually enjoy enough *flow*. Part of this is our inheritance, our bodies and the patterns of worries that we picked up from our parents, and part of it we learned as we went along. Some of our lack of flow is just habit and so we can change it, but some of it is genetic. Contemporary thinkers suggest that we can even change our genetics, and maybe that's true, but even without literally changing our DNA, we can help ourselves by learning to how enhance our state of flow.

When we're not in flow, we are in *block,* which means that there's something going on in our body, mind or emotions that is stopping the flow of energy. When we get sick, it's because there is a block somewhere. Wellness is flow; illness is block. Trust is flow; worry is block. Withholding is block; sharing is flow. Connection is flow; unhealthy isolation is block. Prayer is flow. Kindness is flow. Generosity is flow. Acceptance is flow. Love is flow.

You can use StillPoint to help understand where you're blocked and how to remove the block and restore flow. I believe that health and flow are our natural states. When you're around babies or animals or gardens, you can feel the flow. It's just pleasant and sweet to enjoy the energy they pour out to you. I often feel that the handicapped are more fun to be around than everyday people on the street because in many ways they are unblocked.

After I was divorced, I would sometimes attend community gatherings for the single—mostly dances, as it turned out. Although I didn't really think I could find a soul mate there, I was determined to show the Universe that I was at least trying for one. Most of the time, just being there was painful for me; at 47, I felt like I was a seventh grader again, a gawky homely girlchild not even in the same ballpark with the blond cuties who wowed all the boys. This, I told myself as I gritted my teeth, must be good for me, since it was so uncomfortable.

One evening, after alternating as a wallflower and asking reluctant men who still hated their ex-wives to dance, a young man ran and slid up to me on his knees and asked me for a spin around the floor. When he rose, I saw that he had cerebral palsy and was also somewhat mentally handicapped. This guy had absolute flow. Just touching his hand was pure delight. We danced fast and slow; I started to let go and enjoy myself. "You're doing good," he said to me with a smile, and after we finished dancing he escorted me back to my seat. Sitting there, I understood that I had been experiencing these forays into singledom with a great deal of *block*. I was enduring these social gatherings full of my old emotional patterns. Understanding that, boom! I was ready to let go of the blocks. I walked up to an old friend and asked him to dance. To the wild drumbeats we spun, leaped, and boogied the rest of the evening, and to my surprise, everybody around us started letting go and having a good time, too. Pretty soon a whole section of the room was unblocked and whirling and bouncing together.

Is a state of *block* a bad thing? You may be surprised to realize that it is really not bad in itself. Rather, it's something we can learn from and in many cases it's a blessing.

Sometimes *block* works in a positive way to slow us down. Think back to the last time you got a cold or went down with the flu. If you think about what you were doing at the time, you may realize that you had been overdoing it in some way, overextending yourself, pushing to deal with challenges and not quite getting everything done. Your body created blocks that allowed your immunity to go down, so you got sick and had to stop. That's a *good* thing. A better thing would be to stop and rest *before* we get sick, but since most of us don't choose that, our bodies do it for us. But that doesn't mean our present state of block, our temporary illness, is a *bad* thing. It simply means that our body has created a circumstance for us that will allow healing. That's good.

As another example, most of us have had an experience similar to Jon. He was traveling on a two-lane state highway early one morning, and all of a sudden experienced a big block. He should stop driving *right then.* Like most of us, Jon hesitated for a moment before heeding the block, but it got even stronger: stop driving right now! So Jon quit resisting and pulled over just before crowning a hill. He was shocked to see a huge eighteen-wheeler come tumbling over the hill out of control, weaving over both lanes. If Jon had continued driving, his little Toyota—and he—would have been smashed to bits. So you can see that block is not a bad state of affairs. It may be a message that can save your life in one way or another.

How can you use StillPoint to understand your daily blocks and flows? How can we learn to read them, to move the blocks, to create more flow? The process is actually very simple, and you're ready for the adventure: read on.

In Summary. . .

- StillPoint is a simple body/mind practice that creates a moment of perfect stillness in the body and in the soul.
- Many religions speak of a concept like StillPoint.
- StillPoint gives you peace of mind and ease in your body.
- StillPoint may result from states in the body *and* in the mind or spirit.
- StillPoint is interwoven with intuition.
- When you feel peaceful energy, we may call it *flow.* When we feel the energy stop, we may call it *block.*

Chapter Two: Finding Your StillPoint

Peace, be still. We hear the words, but we don't have a clue about how to go about it.

We assume that our constant mental motion is a modern malady, our relentless racing thoughts, and yet they must have troubled our distant ancestors, too, since all the ancient writings point to the remedy—be still, be still. Evidently our mortal minds are naturally programmed to rush, rush, rush, and unfortunately our modern lifestyle only seems to make it worse. There's so much to fill our minds—email, television, telephones, advertising, errands to run; the endless demands of employment; buying stuff and cleaning it and sending it out to the garbage and replacing it and insuring it. . .well, just thinking about it all makes us feel that we have to get into gear and get busy some more. And yet the answer to it all, including the physical ills that accompany all this noise and stress, is its opposite—stillness.

We were born with the ability to find stillness. We gazed into our mother's eyes, and in that perfect moment of quiet and connectedness, we were still, we were whole, and nothing else mattered. As much as the antibodies in our mother's milk, these beautiful, innate moments of stillness boosted our immunity and kept us well. And like babies, everything in this world sometimes finds stillness, if even for a rare instant—even mosquitoes, even hummingbirds, those incredibly swift creatures. In fact, if you are ever so lucky as to observe a hummingbird at rest on a limb, you will enter into an absolutely miniature delight of stillness.

Throughout the ages, people have been willing to move heaven and earth to find stillness, and certain religious practices, such as Buddhism and Hinduism, have sometimes developed elaborate methods to help their disciples come to stillness. Even today, many of us practice such techniques as meditation and intentional breathing to find healing moments of stillness. No doubt about it, these practices still work, but most of us don't find the time and focus to do them consistently— unfortunately, another symptom of our relentless busy-ness.

That doesn't mean that we cannot find the stillness we need, however. Without long weeks and years of seeking, we can learn some simple ways to find stillness, to create StillPoint, in our lives, and these moments will bring healing, understanding, security, and love into our everyday routine. In fact, after you learn to find your own StillPoint, any time you face a challenge, you can quickly move into that quiet stillness and handle your problems with ease and comfort. Every day you'll enjoy more peace, more health and more love, and it's likely that you'll never be bored again, because every time you find StillPoint, you're certain to find out something new.

Be patient with yourself as you start to learn stillness. It may have been years, decades, since you've experienced it. Think back to your childhood; if you were fortunate and grew up without the constant bombardment of TV and stereo, you will remember many moments of sweet stillness. I can recall lying on a broad branch of an old white-barked walnut in our front yard, the afternoon heat filtered through the thick, barely moving leaves, the bitter scent of the bark and newly forming nut hulls wafting around me. The afternoon passed as if there were no time, and the quarrels inside my home seemed far away; indeed, in those silent, still moments, I felt that nothing unpleasant could touch me, that I was whole, happy and safe. That's something of what StillPoint feels like.

As you get ready to find your own StillPoint, I recommend some preparatory experiences to begin to slow your inner experience. At first, all this may be hard, because our clever, diligent minds want to get busy explain our experiences to us, to help us catalog and categorize and label everything is happening to us.

For example, Karen came to see me one afternoon for a bodywork session. She and I had consulted by telephone, and although she seemed to understand perfectly every item we discussed, she still felt overwrought, uneasy and unsettled. When we got together, it was easy to see why. Karen was a brilliant thinker, and every time we arrived at an insight or understanding, she would immediately try to analyze it, see how she could utilize it in her life, and figure out ways it might help her family and friends. Her brain seized every new insight like a retriever snatching up his prey—and ran just as fast, too. In that moment, she usually lost the full understanding of what she'd just learned and transformed it into something else, an experience of busy-ness and rushing and unsettledness just like the world she lived in.

"You have an extraordinary intellect," I finally told her, "but you possess an even more incredible gift, your compassionate heart. Can you ask your mind to take a nice nap for a little while and let us into your heart?"

We began to work again, and soon she found StillPoint about an important challenge in her life, how much control she was exercising over her teenaged children. At that moment, her mind cranked up and went into interpretation once more. However, together we gently stopped her from her busy thinking and remained still. And there Karen received her first essential experience in StillPoint, a quiet, resonant, whole-body, whole-soul *knowing* of how to live peaceably with her children. We remained in that tranquil place for a while, not speaking, and Karen relaxed and enjoyed profound peace and bodily comfort as she internalized this new knowing. Having had a thoroughgoing experience with StillPoint, Karen practiced going in and out of the experience so she could duplicate it next time. You can learn how to do this yourself.

Preparing Yourself for StillPoint

Here are a couple of exercises that you can use to prepare yourself for StillPoint. Of course, you don't need to go through all this every time you want to use StillPoint. Pretty soon you'll get to the point when you'll be able to get there instantly and access the information you need within seconds. And if you're a camper, a fisherman or a hiker, you may know this preparatory stuff anyhow—slowing your pace down to nature's slow tempo.

Earth Exercises

Although the natural world is full of life and activity, it is even so a place of stillness at the same time, and it can always bring you powerful stillness and serenity. Try some of these Earth Exercises to slow down your tempo, settle your mind, and give you a foundation for finding your StillPoint. In fact, these are perfect exercises for everyday peace. In particular, I'd recommend this Daily Clearing, important if you don't get out on a walk or out to the lake for some fishing.

Daily Clearing

Choose a place in your yard where you can enjoy the plants, the wind in the trees, the soft grass, the singing birds, perhaps your favorite cat or dog. Set out a cushion, chair, blanket or hammock for yourself and settle in. Make sure you're nice and comfortable because your first goal is to sit (or lie) still. Stop your body movement. If you notice that you are jiggling your foot or tapping your fingers, just take a deep breath and let it out, stopping the physical movement. Relax and breathe. When your mind gets busy and thinks about making an appointment, starting dinner, or mowing the lawn, just take *another* deep breath, let it out, and let it go.

Now let yourself *notice* everything going on around you. In a few moments, things you didn't perceive before will begin to enchant you: the glint of sun on a quaking aspen leaf, the shrill whiz of a hummingbird's flight, the robins calling back and forth (you never realized they were having conversations!), the bubble of your children's voices in the front yard. If you hear the phone ring or the fax machine go on, just *notice* it and let it go by, just as the whole sweet world of nature goes by. If you feel your body tensing up at all, breathe again and let it go. Clear yourself.

Jerimy, a colleague at the detention center, is a master at this. He grew up hiking and fishing with his dad, so he had a good start. Every morning he stops by the lake for a half hour of fishing before work. He and his family take vacations outdoors as often as they can. Once when we took our students hiking, Jerimy astonished me by seeing birds, fish and animals that I missed entirely. He could slow his rhythm immediately to see the invisible. The world of nature is full of peace and quiet. These moments of soft breathing and noticing in the natural world can bring you health and give you a profound introduction to the experience of StillPoint. Try to arrange your life so you can sit outside this way often.

Daily Clearing with Water Added

Once a week or so, take your chair or blanket to a river or ocean, lake or stream. Bodies of water can carry us even further toward the sweetness of StillPoint. Do just what you have been doing for your Daily Clearing; quiet your body, breathe in and let out all the tension and worry you may have, and begin to notice everything that's going on around you. In addition to the good things you usually experience in nature, water produces negative ions that dissolve our tension, calm our nervous systems, and eke away our nervous surcharge of energy. It adds a beautiful dimension to your Earth Exercises.

Barefoot Release

Every couple of days, take off your shoes and walk in the dewy morning grass, or if you're lucky enough to live by a beach or river, walk in the sand. They say that your stress and tension leave right out the soles of your feet. While you walk barefoot, do your Daily Clearing—breathing, letting go, and noticing.

Brushing Meditation

If you're so fortunate as to have pets (or children) in your life, every few days take a brush and gently brush their fur (or hair). They'll adore the attention, and you'll be amazed at how it calms and soothes you. When you do this, put aside your plans and worries for the moment, and just concentrate on the experience of brushing and enjoying the beauty of your child or your pet. This is a first step toward *blending,* an important technique for interpersonal problem-solving later on.

Baby Blending

Another delightful way to do this is to hold a baby. Most of us don't have babies in our lives at the moment, but I sometimes go down to the hospital and gently touch the preemies or get permission to hold infants who are sick. Babies are 100% spiritual energy inside a little tiny body. Holding them can bring you an unexpected and amazing blessing of peace and love.

To do this meditation, just hold a baby softly and walk, freeing your mind of all your concerns, feeling the gentle, pure spirit of the child, and giving him or her all your love. Your body relaxes with each step you take, and the baby relaxes, too. As you pour love into the infant, you feel your own soul fill up with the gift of love from the baby. Pretty soon you notice that the baby is nodding off, and you are feeling very soft and relaxed yourself. Babies, like animals, live in a world that has no time, and learning to blend with them can help us to share that experience of timelessness, which is an aspect of StillPoint. It's a gentle gift you can give to exhausted mothers as well, to give them a break as you walk their babies.

Whenever I travel by air, if there's a screaming baby on board, I always offer to hold it and use this technique. There's not a lot of room to walk on airplanes, and I wouldn't want to worry a mother by moving very far away. Still, most mothers traveling with infants have reached their limits, having struggled through ticketing and terminals and waiting for their flight, and most babies have turned very cranky by then, so it's a blessed relief for you to help with the child. It's a perfect combination of giving and receiving, and a marvelous instruction in StillPoint.

Garden Growing Still

Grow something in your garden. If it is winter, put together a little planter by your kitchen sink. If it's spring or summer, get out and dig up the soil, even if you only have a bit of space to plant. Perhaps you live in an apartment and have no soil at all; go get some big pots and fill them with soil and plants, setting them out on the porch or deck. You don't have to make a huge planting, just enough to get you digging and enjoying your growing things. You watch and water and weed them every day, and just as you may have read in the wonderful children's book, *The Secret Garden,* all these changes bring daily delight and revelation. You can find tremendous interest in growing things, as simple as they are, and when you tend them, you may find further peace and quiet that will help you find your StillPoint.

Lying in Stillness

Once in a while, stretch out full length on the sand or grass. Choose a time when it's not too hot (or cold) and just let your body lie full outside on the ground. Close your eyes if you want, and feel the kindness and support of the earth around you. Again, you can combine this with your Daily Clearing.

Physical StillPoint

There's one type of StillPoint which is simply physical. It is very relaxing and can help you take the step toward the full-self StillPoint that we're hoping for. As I've said, StillPoint is partly based on phenomena that happen in the body. CranioSacral practitioners often distinguish between this physical StillPoint and sudden quiet knowing, which they term "Significance Detector", but in this book, I use the terms interchangeably. You can induce physical StillPoint with a little device. Some catalogs sell them, "StillPoint Inducers," and you can buy one easily; just look it up on the Internet. Or, if you like, here's how to make one yourself. Just get yourself a couple of tennis balls and put them inside a sock. Push them right in and tie a knot to hold them firmly in place. Then place the two balls right at the base of your skull, lying down on them. You may use a pillow or not; see what feels best. This simple tool quietens the pulse of your CranioSacral fluid and gives you a kind of StillPoint. It can boost your immunity and help you find and feel stillness.

Methods for Finding StillPoint

Doing your Daily Clearing prepares you for the next step: finding your StillPoint. These are the methods that I have used for years as I have facilitated people in StillPoint. These methods are long tried and true. Most people go to a therapist to benefit from this wonderful treatment, but I have found that you can learn how to do it quite well by yourself, with a little practice and patience.

Two Ways

I have found that some people are kinesthetic (body-based) and some are mental (mind-based). Each one finds StillPoint in roughly the same way, but they experience it differently. I am very kinesthetic, so I use that method with most of my clients. However, sometimes it doesn't work well for someone, who might benefit more from a mental approach.

Kinesthetic

Sit or lie down somewhere comfortable and quiet. Although you will learn to find StillPoint in any place or situation, while you're just beginning, it's important to work in a quiet environment. Take a moment for Clearing. Soon you will feel relaxed and peaceful and increasingly aware of everything around you.

Now check in with your body. Is there anywhere you feel tension or tightness? Place your hand, opened full and soft, on that area. Make sure you don't push down on your body; just rest your hand there. Take the time you need. Many people find tension in their tummies or around their hearts, and if you can't pinpoint another area of tension in your body, both are always good places to begin.

As you lie there with your hand on your body, you may experience some of the following: The tension may increase, or you may feel strong emotions welling up. When that happens, just allow the feelings to come up as they do (don't try to suppress them or stop them). You may ask yourself some questions about them:

- o "Why am I tense?"
- o "What's the source of this tension?"
- o "What am I feeling now?"
- *o* "What is this about?"

Most of the time, a clear answer will run through your head, and at the same time, you'll feel time stop, feel your body go even more relaxed and peaceful, feel a deep, profound connection with all the good in the world around you, and you'll know you've arrived at StillPoint and that your body and soul are giving you a profound gift of healing and answers to your problems.

Here's an example. I have had chronic pain in my shoulders throughout most of my adult life. Having birthed, nursed and raised nine children (well, we're still in the process of raising them), and having divorced, supported the children financially, and then remarried, I have carried a lot of responsibility. One day I decided to work in StillPoint on my shoulder pain. I lay down and relaxed and noticed, as usual, that my shoulder was tight and tense. I reached my left hand around and touched the area, as far as I could. Sure enough, the tension increased. I asked myself, "What is this about?" And clear as day came the answer, along with the deep peace and relaxation of StillPoint, "You're carrying too much responsibility."

"Well," I challenged, "There's not much I can do about that."

We all tend to argue when we get down to the real problem. It is silly, really, because the answers are coming from the truth that's within us, so how absurd it is to argue! And yet almost all of us still do it when we get to the nitty-gritty issues. It's fine if an argument comes up. Just keep yourself relaxed and see if you can stay in StillPoint. Your body is your ally here; it wants to feel better and will help you if you relax and keep your focus.

I stayed in StillPoint and waited for a while. Then my body seemed to relax even further, and the still, small voice of truth spoke within me.

"You've got plenty of people to help you."

I didn't argue this time, though I wanted to explain (whine, really) that nobody helps me, that I was tired of asking for help, that things might not even get done unless I did them myself.

"Your husband and your children will be glad to help. You can make this work. Don't carry this pain anymore. Let it go."

Perhaps the words didn't come just like that, but the understanding did, and as I "got it," a sweet, calm, delicious sensation flowed through my whole body and mind. I rested for a moment, and the pain was gone in my shoulder. Everything felt perfectly still—and in a way, it is, because the CranioSacral rhythm does pause for a moment in StillPoint. When I got up, I felt good all over, and over the next few days I tried asking my family for help—and got it, peacefully and gratefully.

Did the pain ever come back into my shoulder? Yes, it did, because I was not really committed to living a well-supported life. The shoulder pain was a little reminder that I still had some work to do on this issue. However, there are people who complete such a process and never feel that particular pain again.

And it's okay if we still need to work on things over and over, because each time, we get a little better. I remember a student asking Dr. John Upledger, "When do you finally get finished dealing with your 'stuff'?" –meaning our emotional baggage and problems. Dr. John said, "Oh, about seven seconds after your last breath on this earth." In other words, part of the meaning of our life is to get over our "stuff," and that is a lifetime's work. As we do it, we find more and more health, peace, and we often also find ourselves more open to helping others.

As you gain more and more experience with StillPoint, you may feel a gentle pulse as you place your hand on your body. When you reach StillPoint, the pulse will pause, deepen, and go still. The pulse you may feel is your CranioSacral rhythm, based on Dr. John Upledger's concept of the subtle pulse of CranioSacral fluid in your brain and throughout your body. You can use this rhythm as a gateway to finding StillPoint, because when it pauses, you know you're there.

The Mental Type

The process is fairly similar for the mental approach. Relax and get quiet and centered. Then you can ask yourself the question that's on your mind. As you remain still and focused, thoughts may run through your head, and when you come upon the true answer, your body will go very still; some mental types feel that they stop breathing (though they don't) because the CranioSacral rhythm does pause for a moment; everything in your body really does go still. It's almost like a whirlpool or pleasant, crystal-clear tornado inside your body and mind. Your body feels relaxed and comfortable, and you feel peaceful and connected with everything good. You *know* you've got it right.

Here's an example of how this worked for Ron. He had wrist pain off and on for most of a year. Sometimes it would hurt so much that he could hardly function, while other times, he hardly felt it. One day, driving to work, he began thinking through various possible reasons for the pain: carpal tunnel syndrome? arthritis? Then he had a brief flash of a memory of a fall he'd taken months before, trying to pick something up and losing his balance. He realized in StillPoint that he had somehow injured his wrist. Ron made an appointment with an orthopedic doctor who discovered a small, unhealed fracture in the bone. After appropriate medical measures, Ron's pain disappeared and he never had an episode again.

Not Looking For an Answer

You don't need to be seeking an answer to benefit from your deep, whole-self StillPoint. If you're a kinesthetic type, you'll just relax, get centered, place your hand on a tight spot or on your tummy or heart, go into StillPoint, and not seek the answer to any particular problem. The same goes for a Mental type; you'll relax, get centered, and go into a deep, pleasant StillPoint, but not be looking for answers to your questions. When this happens, you may often feel that there *is* an answer floating around, but you don't need to get to it. The experience of StillPoint always is enough in itself. You can enjoy it with your questions unanswered, knowing that you can always find the help you need in another session.

If You Can't Seem to Find StillPoint

If you do your Daily Clearing and perhaps some of the other Earth Exercises, you will most likely be able to find your StillPoint fairly easily, to some degree, right away. However, there are times in our lives when the stress (and distress) becomes so powerful that we may not be able to easily find our way to StillPoint. When this happens, you might like to try a simple technique from Zen practice—counting forwards—or from hypnotherapy—counting backwards. Both ways work well. I particularly like counting backwards, because it seems to cue my body to let go with each succeeding number.

You approach this the same way you do StillPoint generally. Sit or lie relaxed in a quiet space. Focus on letting all tension dissolve, more and more with each breath. When you feel you've relaxed all you can, just tell yourself, "Every time I take a breath, I am letting go more and more. When I arrive at *one,* I will be in StillPoint." Then begin to count. When I'm fairly relaxed, I start at *ten* and count backwards, with every breath letting go of more and more tension. When I'm tense and wound up, I may start at 20. Every time you take a breath, be conscious of releasing tension in any part of your body that's still uncomfortable. In Zen practice, you start at *one* and count as far as you like. By the time you are completely relaxed, you may continue going into StillPoint with the methods above.

If you *really* have a hard time finding StillPoint, don't despair. Go to the phone book and look under Massage Therapy in the Yellow Pages. There you should be able to find practitioners trained in CranioSacral Therapy. These folks are almost always gentle, kind people who will be more than glad to help you. Just tell them you read this book and that you've been having trouble finding StillPoint. I'm sure they'll be delighted to help you on your way.

What You May Experience

As simple as these techniques may seem, I can promise you that they will bring you incredible benefits from the moment you begin—and ever after. You are a vastly interesting eternal soul, and you will find that there is no end to the intriguing things you have to offer, as well as the vast resource of healing you contain within.

Here are some of the ways you may experience your StillPoint.

- You feel relief throughout your body. Your tensions will dissolve, including any particular areas of pain or dis-ease.
- You feel peace throughout your whole self, body, mind and spirit.

- You feel a clear, spinning sense from top to toe, like a crystal tornado or spinning, clear fountain is whirling inside you. This sensation creates more and more stillness, never agitation.
- You feel happy, sometimes so much that you're ready to burst with joy.
- You receive thorough and empowering understanding about a particular problem. Your insights are clear and unmistakable, and they bring you peace and perhaps further solutions to your situation that you may have never considered.
- You feel more compassion and love for those around you. You feel more and more inclined to help people out.
- Occasionally you may experience what Zen practitioners call *makyō.* You may see visions, have spiritual beings visit you, see remarkable vistas, or view dramatic and even frightening images. In Zen practice, you simply allow these manifestations to happen, let them flow through you, and let them go; they do not have particular meaning. From a Jungian point of view, these images rise up from deep within you to present you a message that you may possibly learn from. In Christian mysticism, these images may be a revelation from God.

In my own experience and in helping others with StillPoint, I feel that *makyō* has something to teach us, but it can sometimes be a trap, because we might concentrate on it rather than moving into the quiet experience of StillPoint. As an example, on occasion I have worked with a number of young men who have suffered severe trauma or abuse. They may embark on an extended *makyō* journey full of lights, entertaining images, even full-blown and extended fantasy stories. It is hard to get past these appealing experiences into the real work that we want to do. How might you deal with *makyō* if it should come to you? First of all, you should remember that *makyō* is only a part of the journey, not an end in itself. Remember that it can sometimes become a distraction, and if it does, concentrating on it doesn't serve you well. Keep in mind that *makyō* may come from within your own subconscious and therefore may offer important things, though always somewhat limited things, to teach you as you move *through* it and *into* the healing of StillPoint. In other words, don't get stuck there.

A StillPoint experience may take an instant or some extended time. In any case, when you're complete, you emerge rested, happy, and eager to take on your day-to-day life with renewed zest and a fresh point of view.

Other Paths to StillPoint

Blending

As mentioned above, blending is a wonderful way to enjoy StillPoint. I recommend blending with babies and little children and with animals. Many practitioners are trained to blend with their clients in order to help them, but if you are openhearted in StillPoint and attempt to blend with someone who might be troubled, it can be disturbing. To blend, take yourself into StillPoint while you are in contact with a child or a beloved pet. Open your heart and send your love to her. You will be giving a gentle gift of love, and you may also be surprised at how much love flows back to you.

If you have children, you have probably been blending for years but perhaps didn't realize it. Whenever your child goes out of balance, is feeling sick, or is upset, you put your arms around him and calm him down. In that moment, you may receive a sure understanding of what the problem might be and often a clear feeling of what should be done about it. Smart pediatricians have always known that they should listen to parents who explain what they think is wrong with a child; this surety comes from blending.

The benefits of blending might come from unexpected sources; prepare for some surprises. One year we bought a dozen little chicks, hoping to raise them to hen-hood and enjoy fresh eggs (as well as a lot of amusement). Unfortunately that year, our neighborhood suffered from an infestation of raccoons, and these fellows devoted themselves to doing violence to our chicken flock. We worked hard to secure the old chicken coop, but those rascal raccoons figured out a way in till we finally got it impervious. By that time, unfortunately, we only had one chicken left: Henny Penny, a little black hen. No wonder she was scared and took to roosting on the banister of our front porch! We couldn't let her sleep there, of course; the raccoons would surely get her. So I put myself into StillPoint and gently reached for her, to take her back to the now-secure chicken coop. At first she struggled and squawked, but in a moment, she settled softly into my arms and I walked her back home, talking to her, blending with her. When we reached the coop, before I set her on the roost, I sent her a big dose of love and comfort, and to my absolute astonishment, she sent back an enormous measure of pure, ecstatic love. We remained there in the chicken coop for a moment, swallowed up in a perfectly blended StillPoint, and then she happily hopped to sleep on the roost.

Try It

You can try the calming and centering techniques anytime. And when you're trying to figure out the answers to problems, use one of the approaches to StillPoint and see how it works. Pretty soon it can become second nature to center yourself, go still, and get your answer. Some people say it feels like rotations or undulations in the body; some people just say they feel clear, focused stillness in their mind when they hit on the right thing. Try it out and see how it works for you.

In Summary. . .

- We were born with the ability to find stillness.
- Although there are some complex ways to learn StillPoint, you can learn it quickly and easily.
- Our busy thoughts often interfere with finding StillPoint.
- Being in nature helps us slow down and find stillness.
- Being by water, spending time with pets or other animals, brushing hair, and holding babies can all help us find StillPoint.
- You might use a kinesthetic (body) method for finding StillPoint, or a more mental approach
- If you really struggle finding your StillPoint, book a session with a CranioSacral therapist.

Chapter Three: Everyday StillPoint

"Mom, Dad, I want to go with the basketball team to the state tournament," our sixteen-year-old announced one day.

We disengaged from cooking dinner. "Did you make the team?" we asked.

"No, I just want to go. All my friends are going, and there's room on the bus."

Our first response was to say no, but we didn't know if that was just standard parent mode or something else.

"Let us think about it for a while," we said.

Of course she wanted an immediate yes, but she knew us well enough to let it go for the moment and went off to her room.

We went back to cooking, working together for a while in silence. "So what do you think?" my husband said.

"Doesn't seem right," I said.

"Yes, I'm feeling that this is a bad idea, too," he said.

"OK, so what do we tell her?" Together we figured out some good reasons to give our daughter she couldn't go, but the real reason we said no was that we'd explored the request seeking StillPoint, and we couldn't feel a peaceful stillness about it—we felt "block"—which we took to be a "no."

Using StillPoint in this way makes everyday life much easier. Realizing that the spiritual truth of any particular thing is always present and available, we can stop for a moment, find our StillPoint, and know the right answer, plain and simple. Some people find it through meditation, some through prayer, but in essence the process is similar; we stop, tune in, and when we find the answer, we feel peaceful and sure, often deeply so. When we're still in process of finding the answer, or when we're insisting on *another* answer that we'd rather hear, we feel confused, upset, ill at ease, unpeaceful.

It's especially nice if you can seek StillPoint with your partner or friend, because the stillness seems to increase incrementally when both of you reach it together. When you are feeling blocked and frustrated and can't seem to find peace and stillness, a friend or a therapist can help you. In fact, the times we're completely blocked are the moments we need StillPoint the most.

When I was a single mother, I hoped beyond hope that I could marry someone perfect for me, but I had a hard time really believing it. My friends all told me that the odds were very bad for a woman in her late forties who had nine children. I'd bought a house and settled down to that seeming reality, though deep in my heart I hoped and prayed for a soul mate. I found a book about the subject that recommended going outside and clearly stating your name, residence and availability. I'll admit that it all sounded a little off the wall to me, but I was willing to try anything, so I went into the back yard and announced aloud, "I'm so-and-so, I live in this town in Utah, I'm 47 years old, and I'm looking for you!" Each time I did that, I'd get this deep, powerful stillness that there was someone out there who would be perfect for me. This had a double-edged effect on me. On the one hand, I felt it had to be true and so there was peace in that, but the more obvious truth—at that moment—was that I was thoroughly and unrelentingly alone, eking out a living for my family, fixing the broken toilet, watering the withering lawn.

Not many months after, on an Internet singles website I noticed an entry for a person who looked interesting. Of course I had seen many such entries and started up a number of email friendships, but the results, so far, had been appalling. Besides, this particular entry didn't even have an email listed with it. I passed it by, but as days passed, it kept popping up in my mind and on my computer.

Finally I fixed on the idea of figuring out who this person was. Using clues from his description and his picture, I located him on a small community college campus about an hour from where I lived. I emailed him and he wrote back with some surprise; he thought he'd eliminated himself from the singles website, which he'd only joined in a fit of single abstraction. He *had* eliminated his contact information, but his face and words remained. We started up a charming and wonderful email correspondence and after some months of becoming dear friends, realized that we only lived an hour away from each other. We met and became best friends and then one wonderful night, we fell in love. Now that we knew we had really *found* our soul mates, we didn't want to waste any more time. His name is Russell.

"When do you want to get married?" I asked him one weekend.

"How's Thursday for you?" he said.

"Thursday's great," I said. And so we got married in a friend's garden on Thursday.

This was late summer and we faced the next challenge: moving my multitudinous family across the mountain to a new home. Most of the kids could see that I was happy beyond belief, and although moving was hard for them, they were willing to give it a go. Not, however, our 11-year-old, Joe.

He was playing at a friend's house when we finally loaded up the moving van. The older kids were driving up separately; the little kids were ready to climb into the van. Both Russell and I had this uneasy feeling about Joe. We decided to stop what we were doing and spend a few moments in meditation, to figure out the next step. After a short time, we talked.

I was having a next-to-impossible time figuring out what to do. I'd know, in stillness, that we couldn't force Joe to go with us, and then I'm immediately sail into a thousand different reasons why we really *had* to force him. I couldn't imagine leaving him with his biological father, because I thought that situation would be harmful. I wouldn't consider leaving him to live at a friend's house, yet I couldn't imagine hog-tying him and slinging him into the back of the moving van. I kept trying to contrive ways to force him, though.

As we talked, Russell said, "I don't feel that we can force Joe to go."

"You're right, of course, but maybe we can talk him into it. Maybe there's something that we can do or say that will convince him. Maybe we can bribe him. Maybe it's okay to force him, if it's for his own good. Maybe. . . ."

He just smiled at me and we sat together a little while longer. The only time I felt stillness and peace was when I realized that we shouldn't try to force Joe, whatever happened.

When we drove up to the friend's house, we found Joe in extremity. He was crying as hard as a child could cry, face red, voice hoarse.

I walked up to him and he launched into hysteria. "You can't make me move," he sobbed. "I'm not going. I'll stay with Jason. I'll live on my own. I'll live with Dad. You can't make me."

"Okay," I said. "You don't have to move if you don't want to."

He was so upset that he couldn't even hear what I was saying.

"No matter what you do, I'm not moving!" he continued, on and on.

Finally he heard me when I said, "If you don't want to move, you don't have to. We're not forcing you."

He stopped in mid-sob and just stared. I told him to go on over to his father's house, that he could stay there. I hugged him and kissed him, and we pulled out of the driveway. It was one of the hardest moments of my life, leaving that little guy behind as we drove to our new home, yet even in my grief and pain I could feel stillness and rightness about our choice.

As we settled in and started our new life, our pure joy together was sometimes darkened when we'd think of Joe, living apart and far away. Every day we thought of him and prayed that he'd come stay with us, but so far as we knew, that wasn't likely. Not once did we try to manipulate or force him into changing his mind. In fact, we hardly ever saw him and only talked to him on the phone once a week or so.

Then one day, the telephone rang; it was Joe.

"May I come and stay the weekend with you?"

Forty minutes later, we were at his dad's house and packing him into the car—a world's record of driving the long canyon between the two homes. We passed the weekend calmly and peacefully and took Joe back to his dad's house. Not three weeks later, he called again.

"Do you mind if I come live with you?" he said. It was the middle of the school year, but he made the transition painlessly and has been a delight ever since.

I don't think I could have found peace and stillness without Russell's help that moving day. Sometimes circumstances are just so hard that we need some help. But by following the truth we'd found in StillPoint, that we couldn't force this little boy to do something he didn't want to do; eventually we arrived in a much more whole and stable place together.

StillPoint can make our everyday decision making fairly straightforward and easy. StillPoint can help us make the right decision even when things are confusing. StillPoint can help us say the right thing, choose the right home, make a new friend, find a good repairman, find lost items. StillPoint can take our minds off the mundane by making our choices clear and plain.

The Process

Here's the basic technique for using StillPoint in everyday living.

Once you're faced with a problem or decision, you find a quiet place and either access your CranioSacral rhythm or simply quiet and center yourself (see chapter three for the various approaches to StillPoint). When you are feeling relatively balanced and centered, go through the choices in your mind, one by one, like passing fence posts on a country road. When you reach the right idea or the right choice, you will feel a clear, dramatic moment of quietness, stillness and rightness. You can repeat the process as many times as you like as a way of double-checking the choice you want to make. I almost always go through the process twice or more, just to be make sure.

Be forewarned though; when you feel you've got a lot at stake and you really want a certain outcome, you may resist, argue, or second-guess the answer you get, just as I did when we had to leave Joe behind during our move. This happens to almost everybody when we get answers we don't really want to hear. If you get truly stuck, don't hesitate to find a friend who understands the process or to go to a therapist for help.

Once you've learned how to do this, though, the process doesn't have to take a lot of time. In fact, that's the beauty of using StillPoint in the everyday; you can make good decisions quickly and almost effortlessly. For example, Phyllis and George needed a new car. Their van had overheated early in the summer, throwing a rod and ruining the engine, and they wanted another vehicle to take their family on vacation. They felt a good deal of pressure to replace their van because the kids were almost out of school and everybody wanted to go somewhere for the holidays.

They realized that nobody would want a trade-in with a blown-up engine, so they felt frustrated and backed into a corner.

Then one day, George noticed a newspaper ad about a car sale in a nearby city. The dealership was moving and advertised a big inventory sale, including an offer to accept *any* vehicle as a trade-in. Incredulously George called the company and learned that the offer was real, so the couple piled into their second car, a little sedan, and drove to the city.

There they found a huge lot arrayed with cars, new and used. Overwhelmed by the selection and by the inevitable patter of the used-car salesman, George and Phyllis asked for a few moments of quiet and sat down on the steps of the dealership. They scanned the huge lot together and both felt like looking at the very last row of cars on the further end of the lot.

"Let's go look over there," said Phyllis.

Walking to the far end of the lot, they saw a gold minivan wedged in behind several other cars. Hand in hand, they both felt StillPoint.

"I think that's it," said George. They both checked into their response several times, and both continued to feel peace and stillness when they looked at the car.

"OK, I think we've got it," they said. They walked back over to the salesman. "We'd like that gold mini-van."

"Don't you want to test-drive it?" the salesman asked.

"Oh, no, that's okay," said Phyllis.

"Really, you need to test-drive it," insisted the salesman.

"OK, all right," said George, smiling. They took the keys and went over to the van, driving it up and down the lot briefly. Then they went to sign the papers, including an agreement for a hefty down payment to be covered by trading in their blown-up van. They were very clear that the engine had overheated and blown up, but the company stuck by their promise. George and Phyllis agreed to have the old van towed to the lot Monday morning, signed the papers, and drove away in their new vehicle, which served them flawlessly for years.

When you take on the process of StillPoint in decision-making, however, you need to be willing to hear the answer. The Christopher family had been living in a home that had belonged to their grandmother, and it was too small. The plumbing was going bad, the back steps had recently fallen through, the wiring was antiquated and dangerous, the bathroom fixtures were ugly and old, and everything just felt small and cramped. To fix everything up would take more money than they were willing to spend. It was simply time to move! Collin had just been promoted in his firm, so the time seemed right to find another home.

Collin and Jennifer started looking around the community, then in outlying areas. They kept their realtor busy taking them through house after house. Indeed, it seemed that they walked through just about every possible residence in the area, but nothing felt right. Neither of them wanted to make the wrong choice, but every time they went house hunting, they came home hating their house even more.

This went on for months, for a year, for even longer. Day after day they browsed the real estate ads, but it seemed that they were losing hope. Then one day, both Collin and Jennifer both had the same idea; they'd run down to a competing realtor and look through their listings. They'd never visited this particular realtor before and really had no reason to go there, except just on a hunch. There was an interesting prospect in the rental section.

"I think I've seen this one," said Jennifer. "It's got a pool in the back?"

"No, actually, it's a spa. On a deck? Have you seen it? It's just come on the market," said the realtor.

"Nope. Let's go look."

The home was in a bedroom community near their town, three acres of woods, pasture and a pond. The home was a dream come true, with just the space and simple luxury that the Christophers were hoping for.

"But we don't want to rent," Jennifer said to Collin. The realtor overheard.

"Oh, the owners don't really want to rent this," she said. "We just placed it for rental because the market seems so bad right now and the husband had to take an emergency position out of state."

Discussing the details of the purchase with the realtor, Collin and Jennifer began to realize what a treasure this home would be for them. They knew, deeply and peacefully, that this was the home for them, and the purchase went forward with hardly a hitch. The Christophers finally got what they wanted, but it took a lot longer than they expected. Sometimes the true answer takes time, but it's worth waiting for.

What if you really, truly don't like the answer? Well, there's nothing that says you *have* to follow it. Our experience, though, extensive and sometimes painful, has suggested that in the long run, StillPoint will not let you down. For example, at 18, Abe was graduating from high school and ready to choose a college. He could attend a nearby community college and live at home, go out of state to a larger institution that offered a program he much preferred, or stay with his aunt and uncle and go to a state university with a program somewhat comparable to the one he preferred. The family finances precluded the move out of state, at least at the moment. Mom and Dad wanted Abe to stay at home, of course, and that would definitely be the cheaper choice. Abe took the time to be still and meditate about his choice. He felt StillPoint about going to live with his aunt and uncle, who were glad and willing to have him stay for a year or two.

But Abe didn't want to go there. He hardly knew his aunt and uncle, and he felt uncomfortable moving in with them. Instead, he packed up his stuff and took off to the out-of-state college. There he spent a semester taking classes, working part-time and living off-campus. Although he got student grants and worked hard at his job, he didn't quite make it financially, though he maintained good grades. He got a student loan and ended the semester somewhat in debt.

At Christmas break, he reviewed his choices and concluded that he couldn't make it through another semester financially without incurring more debt, which he felt unwilling to do. He went back through the process and still felt, in StillPoint, that living with his aunt and uncle would be the best. Telephoning them, he learned that they'd still be happy to have him come live there. He enrolled in the state college, maintained his student grant and got a part-time job, and pulled ahead financially as well as academically. He was delighted to learn that the professors in his program were ideal to help him meet his goals, and he found new companionship and love in his extended family.

Was it wrong for Abe to go out of state for the first semester? I would say no, it wasn't wrong. Living with his aunt and uncle remained the better choice, but Abe was free to find that in his own time and way. In other words, we don't *have* to follow what we learn in StillPoint, but in the long run, it works out for the best if we do, because StillPoint is only accessing spiritually what's in our best interest anyway. If a point in time really is a critical factor, most often you'll get this nagging feeling that you need to move more quickly.

When it comes to finding lost items, StillPoint begins to show its immediate usefulness. If you're like us, you are always putting something down and then forgetting where it is. Sometimes it's keys (that's a constant around our house); sometimes it's a bill or an important letter; sometimes it's a book or household item that you need. Needless to say you can spend hours—even most of a day—running around in circles looking for something. You can use StillPoint, combined with a simple skill called scanning, to locate items much more quickly.

Here's how it works. Say that you've misplaced your keys. If you can remain relatively calm, you can use StillPoint to find them. Place yourself in a quiet meditative state and just run through the possible places in your head, starting with generalities: in the bedroom, in the kitchen, out in the car. When you feel StillPoint on a general location, in your mind "scan" the room, that is, visualize all the different places in the room or area, checking for StillPoint as you go. As soon as you know, by your stillness and peace, where the item likely is, you can often walk right to it.

Of course, the catch here is remaining calm. Most of the time when we lose things, we're in a hurry and upset. Recently I misplaced my keys and could not, for the life of me, find them anywhere. I was very worried that I had left them at work, which could cause a considerable risk because the key ring provided entry to just about every important place in my life. I spun around and around the house looking for them. I couldn't even go anywhere in the car because the rest of the family was at work or school. Finally my husband came home and I told him about my dilemma. He did a quick scan—as above—and put his hands on the keys, there in the office, right under a jacket someone had thrown across a shelf.

Similarly, we were looking everywhere in the house for a recording device lent to us by a client. We had held onto his materials for a long time, and he was more than ready to get his belongings back. I looked in his manuscript box; I looked in the garage; I looked in the office; I looked in all our vehicles—nothing. I checked with all the kids; no one had seen it. I checked the storage unit, in all the bookshelves, in all the cupboards—no tape recorder. Then, again, my husband walked calmly out of our bedroom, device in hand. It was under our bed! How it got there I still don't know, since I never used it in our room. Thanks to scanning and StillPoint, he found the device simply and directly.

Being the absent-minded professor as we so often are, I could tell you endless similar stories where we used StillPoint to find stuff. By this time, we're getting pretty good at it. The more I learn about this process, the more I think that professional investigators and trackers must do something along the same line. I remember attending a festival where thousands of people gathered to watch competing dancers. My friends' teenage girl, too young to date but passionately interested in boys, kept wandering away. Finally, during a particularly engaging performance, she saw her chance and took off. She was gone for one hour, two, three. My friends were getting desperate. I decided to try to help and used StillPoint to "track" her. I did the same thing we did at home, scanning in all directions and following when StillPoint indicated a certain way. Sure enough, I followed the path to a parking lot and from there I couldn't get any direction at all. As it turns out, the young lady went to the parking lot with some boys and took off with them in their car. She returned after another hour or so, facing the wrath of her parents, though otherwise safe and sound. Her story corroborated what I'd tracked down in StillPoint.

This somewhat lighthearted story illustrates another more serious use of StillPoint for parents. As our kids grow up, more often than we like we face the frustration of not knowing where our kids are. Maybe the ten-year-old has gone off to visit someone but we don't know who; maybe the sixteen-year-old has taken the car on an unauthorized trip; maybe we haven't heard from the college student in a long time. It's easy to get upset. Possibly the distress is warranted, but how can we know for sure? In such a case, finding StillPoint can be a lifesaver, not only for the peace of mind of the parents but in some cases, for the safety of the child.

Miriam hadn't come home from school, and as we called around, we found she wasn't at the homes of her usual friends either. The hours went on, four o'clock, five, six and still no Miriam. Like most parents, I started to get upset, first a little, then a lot. Pretty soon I found I wasn't thinking straight. Then I remembered; I calmed myself and tried for StillPoint; either Miriam was safe or she wasn't. I settled right down and felt StillPoint that she was just fine. Within the next hour she breezed in; she'd stopped at her friend's house on the way home from school for hot chocolate and cookies and ended up talking for hours. Of course we went over the guidelines for what to do when we stop somewhere after school, but in the meantime, I was spared some needless anxiety and she was spared some of the intensity that would have built had I not felt she was okay.

There's another straightforward, practical way to use StillPoint—when things go wrong with the house and need repair. Most of us spend hours agonizing when something breaks or malfunctions, and sometimes the repairman spends hours, too, trying to pinpoint the problem. However, using StillPoint, you can often figure out what's wrong and even fix it yourself.

When we bought our home, we inherited an ancient hot tub, a throwback to the seventies. The thing works, most days, and provides hours of endless comfort and relaxation. However, once in a while, everything goes skeewhompus; the temperature rises sky-high or algae from outer space start proliferating there. One day, I went out to get into the tub and found that it registered 119° F and was still pumping out heat. I reached over and pulled out the plug to just stop the monster and then, a few moments later, plugged it back again (all you electrically savvy folk know that was the wrong move, but I didn't). No response, no juice. I was dismayed; had I broken the thing? I felt we were in no position to replace the hot tub, however much we loved it and used it. What should I do?

After my initial alarm, I sat myself down to think about it. Was the tub itself broken? Didn't seem like it. Thermostat broken? No. Electrical outlet? No. Threw a fuse? Ah, yes, StillPoint. I maneuvered my way to the switch box and flipped the fuse back on. That restored power to the outlet but the tub was still dead as a doornail. What was wrong, what was wrong? I fiddled with the thermostat for a while—no go. Finally I got the idea that there might be a reset switch, like the one on a dishwasher. Of course I couldn't find any such thing on the hot tub, but I called up a friend who knew plumbing and asked him. Sure, he said, the switch was right on top of the motor, just inside the door. I went outside, found it immediately, pushed it, and voilá! The tub switched itself back on! By calming down and using StillPoint to figure out the problem, rather than screaming to a plumber, I saved myself a bundle of money and most of all found a new peace of mind. We could figure out household breakages even if we didn't know much about things.

We soon had occasion to try out the technique again. One day the children rushed upstairs, frantic, because there was water dripping from the ceiling. In an older house, as you know, plumbing disasters can escalate from horrible to catastrophic, and you never know what's going to happen with your slightest move. One twist of a pipe and the whole shebang can fall apart, as our sad experience had already taught us. Your first thought is always that a sewer line has popped and is propagating disease straight into the downstairs carpet. I'm always tempted to fly into a panic, but my steady-on soul mate calmed me down to think about things a bit. We scanned through the possibilities. Sewer line? No (thank God). Water line? No (that's strange; what then?). Someone had just been in the shower; was it the drainage pipe? No . . . Russell figured it out; there were hairline cracks in the shower tile, and one of the kids' long showers had leaked enough water through the fractures to sprinkle through the ceiling. The downside of this, of course, was that we couldn't fix it right away, but the upside was that we could get the kids to limit their shower time (always a good thing generally) and avoid the problem for the time being. This was a much better alternative than twisting pipes or unnecessarily employing an expensive plumber.

Of course there's always the chance that you'll need to employ a professional. Last spring the water trap in the basement overflowed, and we had no clue about what could be causing it. We are on a septic tank system and we knew that whatever was wrong could only get worse, not better. We considered all sorts of home remedies, but finally settled on calling Roto-Rooter. Sure enough—it was roots! The ubiquitous Chinese elms that populate our property had sent down roots straight into the septic tank pipes. The Roto-Rooter man informed us that our best bet would be to take down the offending trees, or the problem would keep growing, along with the roots. Several days later we were minus several Chinese elms, had installed some new sections of pipe, and never had a moment's trouble since.

You can use StillPoint to address just about every concern that might come along in your life. For example, if you find yourself needing to earn some extra cash, you could plug away at a moonlight job at a minimum-wage job and fill in the gap—or you could do some brainstorming, with the help of StillPoint, to access some more efficient ideas. Typically, when you're strapped for cash, it's hard to think straight and clear, so you may need to spend some time calming down and thinking through, and even making a list of, all possibilities. Usually you can use some talent or belonging that you already have to bring in some money.

For example, Zarah, ten years in the U.S. from Turkey, had grown up belly dancing, but for years hadn't performed or used her talent. She spent one afternoon talking with a friend, going over the possibilities of getting a job, but she lacked skills, confidence and language ability to feel comfortable getting a job in her new country. As the two friends wrote a list of all the possible jobs Zarah might get, she grew more and more discouraged, till she wrote down "belly dancing." Zarah's friend pointed out that belly dancing was having a new birth here in the United States and that people were clambering to get a chance to try it. Zarah had a peaceful, calm feeling that this was a good idea. Within a week, she had a class of eight people all signed up, each of them paying $10 a week for the privilege of dancing with her. As luck would have it, Zarah had a good hardwood floor right in her family room, so with some cooperation from her family, she started up a productive studio right in her home, investing little time and no money, since she owned plenty of belly dancing tapes already. Soon she had saved up the money she needed to enroll in college and pursue her dream of becoming a pediatric nurse.

Similarly, when he was growing up, Bruce was a real computer geek. In his spare time he taught himself the program C++ and other programming languages, just for the intense joy of learning them. He spent long hours perfecting his skill of creating graphics, websites, and other computer programming skills. When he went to college, he realized that he needed to get a part-time job in order to survive, and began visiting the student employment center looking for possible positions. Everything he saw felt like such a bad fit, and he dragged his feet from interview to interview, secretly hoping that he wouldn't get any of the positions available. And sure enough, he didn't. Half relieved and half dismayed, he started discussing his situation with a friend. Imagine his surprise when this friend, who in the meantime was staffing a start-up business of his own, offered Bruce an excellent position in programming even before he graduated from college. Bruce's specialized interest helped him sail through his degree; in fact, his only frustration was keeping his number of work hours down enough to complete his class work. Although this is not a story specifically illustrating StillPoint, it shows that we can receive clear resonance on the path we should take in life.

In my life, I have always been a teacher, first and last, but when I started having children, teaching fulltime became impossible. I took a part-time position at our local university, but even that proved to be too much by the time my third baby was born. I needed—and wanted—to earn some extra money, but I couldn't wrap my mind around any job that would take me away from my little children and my newborn. Still, I had spent many hours correcting essays and even many *more* hours reading and writing, so my editing skills were excellent, just from the practice.

From a colleague I learned that the university press was looking for part-time editors to work freelance out of their homes. Even though I had never heard of StillPoint before, bingo! I had a clear, calm feeling that this was for me. I went to the office to take a practice test to measure my skills. The head of testing returned shortly with the outcome, with a severe expression on his face. He determined that I had cheated on the exam because I had a perfect score. I assured him I hadn't cheated at all and offered to take a similar test again, with him watching! From this simple beginning I built a business doing freelance editing and writing that lasted all the years of my childbearing and –rearing, the time my kids were big enough that I could get back into teaching.

You hear variations of this story again and again, when people go through all the options and clearly hit upon the perfect one. This works not only for a part-time income supplement, but also of course in choosing a career. In fact, it makes career choice so much easier. The truth is that sometimes we often take on work for the interim, although it is not really our life's work. Eve was 21 and just starting her education. She had gone through several unproductive diversions along the way and lost some time between high school and this new start for college, and now she was ready to begin. Eve had a natural talent for creating beautiful hairstyles, but her real interest lay in assisting troubled teenagers, as she had been when she was younger. At present, though, she was facing at least six years of intensive education and no visible means of support. Thinking through her present options, she wrote down her choices: work till she saved enough money; live on student loans; work part-time (and not really make it financially); forget college and try to get a good job without a degree; and—surprisingly—get *another* kind of degree, a short-term degree that would easily let her survive while she pursued her further goals. That degree, she reasoned, would obviously be in cosmetology because she was such an excellent hair designer. As she went down through her list, she got an absolute StillPoint on the final option. Of course, like most of us, Eve wanted to resist that one, because it felt like such an unnecessary diversion from her main goals. Over several months of summer vacation spent resisting and checking in again to see if it was *really* true, Eve finally got herself enrolled in Cosmetology. There she was astonished that she qualified for a great deal of student aid, enough to pay her expenses and even live comfortably as she acquired her new skills. She worked part-time at an exclusive salon during her undergraduate years, earning a comfortable living and enjoying the side benefit of talking to many teens along the way and counseling them informally—a great source of experience in her chosen field!

Try It...

Before long—even today—you are going to have to make a decision, a small one (where to eat lunch or what to buy your mom for Mother's Day) or a big one (what job to take or what's going wrong with your car). In the moment you realize you've got to decide, let yourself stop for a moment and go through the choices. Maybe you'll write them down; maybe you'll just run through them in your head. Then use the techniques in Chapter Three to calm, center and access your natural rhythm. Take your time; make it easy. Once you're calmed and centered, go through the list of choices once more. I almost can guarantee that one of the choices will bring StillPoint and you'll know what's best for you. If you aren't sure, just do it again and pay attention to your experience.

As I've said, it often happens that we dislike the choice that's right, and then we resist it and start making up every kind of argument for that *not* to be the choice. This is natural and you should expect it, and of course you always have the choice to refuse and choose something else. In the end, though, this is usually counterproductive because the information we gain in StillPoint comes from our own spirit accessing the truth that exists in the spiritual world all around us. You've likely got this right. Take your time and think through all your arguments and understand that resistance is normal (though usually futile).

In Conclusion

From day to day, there's probably no more valuable skill than StillPoint for making life go smoothly and easily. Instead of bumbling through many inappropriate choices, we can find StillPoint on what would be ideal for us and go through that. I believe that many people naturally take this approach with choice making, but that also many of us scramble in confusion and waste much time and personal energy on things that could be simple and straightforward. It's worth the time and effort to calm down and find StillPoint, which will always aim us in the right direction.

In Summary . . .

- Sometimes we need our partner or a friend to help us with StillPoint.
- Using StillPoint can help us more easily make everyday decisions.

- StillPoint is not an imperative; you don't *have* to follow the feelings you get in StillPoint, although things often work out better when you do.
- You can use StillPoint to help you find lost or misplaced items.

Chapter Four: StillPoint and Your Relationships

"He was my soul mate," said Karla, stirring her coffee and not looking up at me. "I just know he was. But we couldn't make it work. Every time we turned around, we were arguing. But we were so perfect for each other! I don't think it's possible to have a good relationship anymore."

Sound familiar? When it comes to personal relationships, living together, having children, being close to each other, we often struggle more than with anything else in our lives. Why should this be so? I think it's because being together, loving each other, and dealing with everyday problems bring out the character traits we're still trying to refine. Fortunately, StillPoint can be an easy and liberating way to grow in our relationships. With StillPoint, we can figure out why we're attracted to certain people. We can see if those attractions can bring relationships that will be vibrant (and safe) for us. When we run into conflict or obstacles along the way, StillPoint can help us understand what's really going on and get out of our limited point of view so the disagreements can move into harmony and progress for both of us. We can know what to say to our kids, our colleagues and most especially our partners, especially when the heat rises and more than ever we need to know how to get along.

Soul Mates

Just about everybody talks about soul mates, but what are they actually saying? A soul mate is someone who seems to vibrate on the same string, so to speak. We may feel like we knew each other all our lives. We feel like we step together in harmony as if we've never been apart. We love to touch, talk, and just be with each other. Often our goals and aspirations are so similar. We almost feel like we're in each other's mind, thinking each other's thoughts.

Yet after we've lived together for a while, nuisances and disruptions so often make all this magic disappear. Here are a couple of ideas on why this might be so. The first important question you can ask yourself in a relationship is whether you're in a connection of "opposites attract" or "birds of a feather flock together." Typically, young love (at no matter what age; maybe "first true love" would be closer) transports us full-blown into "opposites attract," since we often find ourselves drawn to someone who resembles one of our parents, typically the one who most controlled or dominated us. When you're in an attraction to an opposite, the magnetism can seem almost irresistible, because you're responding to cues you picked up when you fell in love with your mom or dad as a child. This, by the way, is normal and just about everybody goes through it; you know: "Mommy, I'm going to marry you when I grow up."

As an example, Justin had been through two long-term relationships that ended badly. Both times he thought he knew the woman well, but when they finally lived together, he felt that they were withholding, cold and judgmental. Whenever they disagreed, his partner would invariably stop speaking, break off sleeping with Justin, and avoid any kindness or contact with him. Justin had been alone for two years now and didn't know how to proceed. As we talked, I asked him about his mom.

He blushed a little and looked away. "Yeah, she's like that too," he said, "and so's my dad, really. I always wanted it to be different. Sometimes our house felt like a deep freeze and I always felt like it was somehow my fault. If I just tried a bit harder, I could make it right."

Justin realized that he was "marrying his mother" every time he got into a relationship with this type of woman. He entered the relationship with the emotional pattern that attracted and sustained these relationships. In a way, it's like wearing one of those "Hit Me" signs that we tape on each other's backs as little kids. Of course, realizing this and doing something about it can be two different things. It took Justin a few years of living alone and sorting out his emotional baggage before he was ready to get together with someone different. Fortunately, after some time, he finally met a woman he could communicate with and make a relationship that worked.

In contrast, the "birds of a feather" kind of attraction puts you together with someone who is indeed similar to you in nature. This can be great when your life reflects beliefs and behaviors that are clear and positive, but often there's a big gap between what we *say* we believe and what our emotional patterns still are.

As an example, Judith kept repeating this particular pattern. She'd meet a man and feel immediate, strong attraction. After going out together for a while, she'd sleep with him and perhaps move in together. Not long after, Judith's new boyfriend of the moment would start to be more and more controlling and dominant. He'd jealously demand where she'd been, how she'd been spending her money, and why she hadn't called him hourly. The sexual relationships almost always turned to domination and some cruelty. Judith kept saying that she just didn't understand why she was always getting together with abusive men.

Looking further, though, Judith revealed that she had the same tendencies herself. She'd demand that her coworkers cover her shift when she had another appointment; she grew angry when her lovers spoke to other women, however innocently; she refused to do everyday tasks that she felt were beneath her. At first, realizing these things about herself made Judith very uncomfortable; in fact, she could hardly bring herself to look at the truth squarely. When she did, however, Judith saw right away how she might change her life so she was so much less controlling. After time, she began to attract friendships and then love relationships that were supportive and non-abusive.

So look at your own relationship. Is it "opposites attract" or "birds of a feather"? Say it this way: "This relationship is based on the attraction of opposites," and then, "This relationship is based on commonality." StillPoint will reveal the answer. Go through the statements a few times so you can see how you're feeling and responding to your answer. Knowing this basic dynamic will take you to the first step of making your partnership work, because the "opposites attract" type of relationship will almost always leave you feeling that you're living with a creature of an alien species. Of course, this is neither good nor bad; it will just be the way of your relationship and it will require focus on good communication skills. The "birds of a feather" relationship will require you to maintain good boundaries and to avoid blaming the other person for everything that goes wrong, because most of the time, that person is really a mirror of your very own self.

You need to keep in mind, though, that the chemistry of falling in love is extremely powerful, but that it always, *always* changes after a while. If we don't understand that, we will be eternally disappointed in our relationships. When we fall in love, we feel powerful chemistry: our tummy jumps, our heartbeat accelerates, we get short of breath, and we're intensely motivated sexually. These strong feelings are so pleasurable that sometimes we're deeply disappointed when they change after we win each other's love. In fact, many people go from relationship to relationship trying to find and recreate that huge rush of passion and pleasure that we get when we fall in love. Of course, in a long-term committed relationship, we can fall in love over and over again, but have no doubt: for every up there is a down; for every joy, a sorrow, and nothing is so predictable of that as relationship.

Most of us don't *really* understand that the way we relationship (and really the way we experience our whole world) has everything to do with the way we grew up, how our family was, how we were educated—in short, how we have had our "operating system software" installed. Most of us assume that we see the world in a very clear way, and that there's not much choice about it, but that is simply not true. Everything we've experienced throughout our lives has created our "software;" you can call it your ViewPoint. Other writers have compared it to the glasses through which we see the world. The wonderful thing about software is that it can be changed or reprogrammed, and we can always reboot with a new program. In other words, by taking a different point of view, we can "change our mind." Once you understand this simple principle, it can change your life—and your relationships—forever. To understand this, consider these two stories.

Once I was working a business deal with a lady who was quietly, calculatedly defrauding me. At some deep level, I must have known this was happening, but I refused to listen to those inner warnings and instead chose to trust her. She told me that the local bank had embezzled part of our funds, but that the bank president had asked her to say nothing about it till they got the federal agencies to investigate the situation. (Pretty dumb of me to believe that, but that's the story.) Every time I drove by that bank, I felt violated, angry and suppressed because I believed that I was being dealt with unjustly. When I finally got to the bottom of this lady's dishonesty, however, I realized that all those negative feelings about the bank were a fabrication! Nothing wrong had gone on at the bank, and I had no need to feel angry or frustrated! My ViewPoint had created some pretty strong feelings that were very real, yet baseless in reality.

Here's a happier illustration of the same concept. Two friends came together one night to talk. Both of them had gone through some hard times in their lives; he had been through a series of painful gay relationships, and she, although straight, had also run through a chain of boyfriends who had mistreated her. They had been dear friends over the years, though, and were a good example of the "birds of a feather" kind of attraction. As the night progressed, they grew closer and closer, and ended up having sex.

When they woke in the morning, they realized that something new and untoward had changed their world. Far from being stuck in one single point of view, they were shocked that they could alter their ViewPoint even on these powerfully basic issues of gender and attraction. After a few soul-wrenching days apart, they got together.

"What if we acted as if we were in love?" they said to each other. "What if we were tender, kind, sweet, passionate and caring for one another, like lovers?" They decided to give tit a try. And it worked: they fell in love, and not long after married and had children together. They've stayed together and they're still living in love, all because they were willing to shift their ViewPoint.

This story is not about gender issues but about the couple's willingness to open their minds and hearts and change their ViewPoint, being willing to allow their soul mate to be someone they didn't expect. We can also call this "changing your mind" — a basic, foundational change in the way we see the world.
It may be hard to accept, because we all invest a great deal in the strength of our opinions, yet much of what we feel or believe is created by the way we see the world.

And the way we see the world is a *choice*. It may not always seem that way, but in most cases, it is. At first, this may seem to be a very difficult concept, because none of us enjoys feeling like we've got it wrong. It's worth the time and effort to re-examine the way we see the world. Whether we like it or not, not one of us grew up in a perfect home, and the ViewPoints we absorbed as children influence just about everything we do as adults.

If you're not totally convinced about that, try this simple exercise. Using the techniques in Chapter Three, find a quiet place and make this statement: "The way I see the world is the way things really are." Most people—including myself—do *not* get a clear StillPoint on that. This begins a new journey to some interesting—and fun—and fundamental changes in the way we behave in relationships, and it can open the door to a lifetime of love with your soul mate.

Probably one of the most pervasive mis-beliefs in our world has to do with a concept we might call *hierarchy;* you can also call it competition. In this ViewPoint, somebody's always *right,* so somebody else ends up being *wrong.* Somebody wins; somebody loses. Somebody teases; somebody else is teased. In this world, you are always on edge in case you make a mistake and you will be *wrong.* Somebody gets an A; somebody else *must* get a C, so not as to mess up the curve. We could choose instead to live in a world in which it would be possible for everyone to get an A, where everyone would pull together for all to succeed.

Many women live in real fear of criticism, of being found to be *wrong.* In fact, they often steel themselves for the next perceived attack. However, this is not a problem just for women. It's the same for men; just consider the ever-touchy male ego that will not bear criticism. So many of us—men and women—participate in the big put-down game, often couched in humor. Only we all know that these put-downs are not funny at all. Instead they reflect an inappropriate ViewPoint that you gotta win or you're gonna lose.

Here's the deceptively simple solution: Even if you *want* to win, choose *not* to win. In relationships, choosing to not win is one of the most freeing concepts I have ever found. Perhaps the phrase should be reworked like this: If you want your *relationship* to win, choose to let your partner win all the time. It has been my experience that almost nobody thinks they are competitive, driven to win by our culture's programming.... but virtually everyone is.

No doubt you've got a million arguments running through your head about why this won't work. Before you set them in stone, run this statement through your mind with the intent to check it with StillPoint: "Choosing *not to win* will improve my relationships." Just about everyone I know who's tried it has agreed—it works. However, knowing this and doing it can be two very different things. If you're game for it, try this little experiment tonight (assuming you're in a relationship). Challenge your partner to some meaningless game, a short one or a series of short ones, like tic-tac-toe or checkers. Then choose to let your partner win; do it subtly, so he or she doesn't catch on. Pay attention to what you feel as you begin to *lose.* If you are like most people, you may feel that urge to compete rouse its ugly head. But if you can stay with it and let your partner win, a remarkable thing will happen. As you see the smiles or twinkling eyes of your soul mate, you realize that you have both just won. It is very empowering to give up the need to win.

If you're not in a relationship right now, it works the same with a colleague, one of your children, or a good friend. And here's the next step. If you are getting convinced that you are really not competitive, put yourself to a truer test. Think of one of those many little ongoing battles in your relationships, one of the fairly insignificant ones, like what color to paint the family room. She may want mauve or something trendy. He may want architectural white, just like in those homes in *Architectural Digest*. Quietly bring up the subject with your partner and choose not to win. Just say the words out loud: "You know, if it would make you happy, let's paint the room mauve this weekend." The freedom comes the moment you realize that ultimately *it really doesn't matter* what color the family room is. People fight about such things all the time, sometimes for years. The interior decorating becomes a huge issue, a disagreement that separates us from each other. What we *lose* in such battles—unity and closeness with the ones in the world who matter the most to us—is always much more than what we *win.*

Once the family room is mauve, the moment of truth will present itself soon enough. You will have the opportunity to choose not to win on a more long-held conflict, or you may be challenged with a serious mistake by your partner. As soon as you can squelch the impulse to say that delicious phrase: *I told you so,* you will begin to find the power to be a true soul mate.

I would add a small disclaimer here. I'm not saying that you should surrender your will and negate your opinion all the time. But I am saying that we can give up our driving need to be right, to be in power, to always win. One real symptom of competitive thinking is blaming. If we are honest, most of us have almost a knee-jerk reaction for blaming our partner or colleagues when things go wrong. Blaming is a way of taking away that horrible feeling that we're the one that lost while someone else won. It's a way of diverting the emotional sting we feel when things go wrong and we know there's going to be trouble for someone—and we do everything we can to make sure it's not *us.*

To help you with those dreadful moments when you're mad enough to spit out words that could hurt someone, here's a simple exercise that can serve you throughout your life. It's very powerful, again, one of those things worth the whole price of admission.

The Three Questions

When you're ready to explode at your partner, child or colleague, make yourself step back for a moment, get as calm and centered as you can, and ask yourself three questions. Go through all the possible answers you can think of. When you hit upon the best one, you will find peace and quiet—StillPoint—and you'll know what to do from there. Unless you are in a life-threatening situation (and you will almost never be), you have the time to take a deep breath, stand or sit quietly, ask these questions:

- "What is really going on here?"
- "What am I truly feeling about this?"
- "What is the best thing to do?"

Suppose that it's Saturday night and you're on the way out to a party. And, once again, your partner is "making you late." You feel your blood pressure rising, and you certainly hear your voice rising in volume as you urge him or her to hurry up so you won't be *late!* There's no way around it; you're already behind schedule; it's time to deal with the situation as it stands.

Before you say a word, stop. Ask yourself the first question, "What is really going on here?" Go through lots of different possibilities in your mind as you seek a clear, non-competitive, non-hierarchal view of the situation. If you find yourself blaming, you probably haven't found the true answers yet. You may get some surprising input: "He's feeling sick," "She can't find her checkbook," "He's worried about the baby," "She doesn't really want to go tonight," or even, "This party isn't the way we need to spend the evening." Once you get StillPoint on an answer, you can proceed to the next question.

"What am I truly feeling about this?" At first you may come up with lots of cutthroat, blaming responses: "It's wrong for us to be late again!" "She's always late to everything!" "He always makes me late!" Take a breath and tell yourself you're not going to blame your partner any more. Notice if you feel the tightness and tension in your body, and consciously let it go. Then you may begin to understand how you're really feeling: "I'm embarrassed when we arrive late," "It makes me look like I'm a bad person," "Everybody stares at us when we come in late," "I don't want to be judged." It may not always be comfortable, but StillPoint can give you to understand right away what's really going on in yourself, and in less than a heartbeat, you can turn yourself around and choose to feel more peacefully about the situation.

Then comes the next question: "What is the best thing to do?" The answer may surprise you, because it may fly in the face of everything you've ever done before. Perhaps you will feel that you should pause, walk over to your partner, and hold him or her gently. Or you may feel that you should sit down and hold hands for a while. You may feel that you should silently pitch in and do the dishes or some other task that's weighing heavily on your partner. You may even feel that you should hang up your coat and not go at all. StillPoint will take you to the right decision, and that will be best for both you and your partner.

When you "change your mind" about winning, when you give up your need to compete, you will suddenly find that there are rarely only two sides to a question. So many arguments start because both people dig a trench for a particular ViewPoint, firmly planting themselves inside, whether or not they even truly believe it! When we give up our need to win, in most cases we can find a number of different ways to solve problems.

For example, Susan and Henry were preparing to buy their first home. They had visited what seemed to be dozens of houses in the area, and found several that fit their needs exactly. The one that they liked the best, however, needed some repairs to make it livable. With a toddler and a full-time job, Susan felt that she could hardly be expected to remodel a home. Henry felt, however, that the price was right and the house was ideal. Without a thought, they both took up arms and began the battle. Then, all of a sudden, Harry backed down. "If you feel that we can't renovate this home, well, I understand how you feel," he said. "We don't have to buy this house if you don't want to."

Susan fell silent and then found herself saying, "You know, it's really the house I love the best of all our choices."

"Me, too," Henry responded. He took her hand and they sat together, silent, for a few moments.

"Maybe we could find a way to do this," Susan began. "My brother is good at fixing things; I know he'd come and help out."

"That's a good idea," Henry said. "And if we could find a way to get some help caring for the kid, you and I could enjoy some time working on it too." From there, the couple talked about various ways to make the situation succeed, and at the end of the discussion, they felt peace and renewed love and commitment to each other. And *that* is when you really win!

The Fourth and Most Important Question

If sometime you find yourself getting madder and madder as you disagree with your partner or colleague, stop yourself, breathe more easily, take a look at the other person, and ask yourself, "What really matters here?" It takes practice to get to some peaceful answers, but in the long run, you will find yourself realizing that **nothing much *really* matters**—except making good relationship. At first you will hear yourself saying, "But we need to balance the checkbook once a week!" "But she is spending too much money!" "But we just have to have a new car!" "But I don't like it when he says *f*---!" Perhaps all of those things are very true. Still . . .ask yourself, "What really matters here?"

Brenda, just beginning a new job and the mother of two small children, had bought an airline ticket to visit relatives on the other side of the country. At this point, the family had little money to spare, and Brenda had saved up for this trip over many months. Some days before it was time to leave, her three-year-old daughter got sick, and then sicker and sicker. The doctor diagnosed it as a serious pneumonia. What should the couple do? Their child absolutely needed both parents to see her through this illness. The ticket was nonrefundable.

"What are we going to do?" she anguished. "Desireé is so sick! I'm scared."

"Maybe you ought to just stay and we'll both take care of her."

"But what about the ticket? That cost two hundred dollars!"

"I know." This was a moment to ask, "What really matters?" What really mattered was the life-and-death situation for their little girl. Of course, you may not always face dramatic situations like this one, but the process remains the same. When you ask, "What really matters?" you eventually come up with the obvious answer, "*Nothing* really matters, not really, except the love and trust we have for each other." You can deal with losing a job, losing a wallet or losing a home, but you can't *ever* afford to lose a loving relationship.

Say Less

One wise marriage counselor pointed out, "If you were planting a garden in the spring, would it help for you to stand around and yell at the tomatoes and corn to grow faster and better?" It's a good comparison, your relationship and a garden; both take a long time to mature, each changes every day, and both bear good fruit with time and care. If you're like most people, as soon as you have a difference with someone, especially your partner, you want to tell them *exactly* and *everything* about what you think and how you feel. If they don't come around to your point of view right away, you want to say it louder and more strongly till they get it!

Instead of escalating, you can choose to say less. Stand back from the situation, make yourself stop talking, and ask yourself the three questions. Sometimes just quietly listening to your partner can stop a disagreement right in its tracks. In fact, Mother Theresa once said, ". . .the fruit of love is silence." I take that to denote loving, kind silence, not mean-spirited, withholding silence (of course).

Taking Care of Babies and Children

Not everybody has children, but lots of us do, and taking care of kids, especially when they're small, can make us feel helpless and clueless. Little ones—and often, bigger kids too—can't always tell us what's going on with them. Yet being a parent, whether you gave birth or adopted your children, gives you powerful feelings for your kids *and* the gift of tuning in and figuring out what they really need. StillPoint can be your priceless aid with this.

Tonya and Reed just had their first baby, a little boy they called Mac. By the time the baby was two months old, all three of them were ready to admit defeat and call it quits. Mac screamed all the time he was awake, and that seemed to be most of the time. Nobody was getting any sleep, and there's nothing quite as desperate as a sleepless parent. Tonya was breastfeeding the baby and being careful with her diet so she wouldn't contribute to colic, but nothing seemed to help. A friend suggested CranioSacral therapy, and the couple—desperate as they were—felt a calm peace that at last they might be able to find an answer.

The couple brought the baby in to see my friend Margot, a CranioSacral therapist who's particularly gifted with babies. As she worked with the infant, she turned and asked the mother, "Was this a straightforward delivery?"

The couple glanced at each other in despair. "No," Tonya answered. "I was deeply sedated and they had to take the baby with forceps."

"I was there," added Reed. "I felt so sorry for my wife and it was terrible watching them pull Mac out with the forceps. It had to hurt him!"

"I think that's what the problem might be," said Margot, as StillPoint confirmed their words. "Let's see . . ." She began to work gently on Mac's head. Before long, Margot could feel encouraging movement in the bones of the baby's head. She continued working with him with that peculiarly gentle touch of CranioSacral work. "We don't always know how these things affect babies," she told the parents, "but we'll see how it goes."

Reed and Tonya took their baby home, and although he didn't stop crying completely, his long screaming sessions ceased. They were ever grateful that Margot was able to help them through this problem.

It's good to be able to get help when you need it, but sometimes you'll have to figure things out on your own. When our boy Joe was nine or ten, he would get night terrors. If you've never seen this condition, you have no idea how horrifying it can be. The child wakes in the middle of the night screaming. He doesn't see or hear you, no matter what you say or do. He trembles, shakes, even convulses. He screams on and on, words that you can't answer: "Mom! Dad! Where are you? It's coming, it's coming! It's so fast, I can't get away!" Stuff like that. The third or fourth time Joe did it, we grabbed him and rushed him to the emergency room. As soon as he woke up, he stopped screaming and remained his good, calm self all the way to the hospital. They couldn't find anything wrong with him other than a mild fever, so they sent him home with me, saying that it was just night terrors and that kids grow out of it, nothing to worry about. As soon as we got home and Joe went to sleep, the problem started up again. We tried waking him up and giving him a drink, thinking that perhaps he was dehydrated because of his fever, but it all continued throughout the night.

Next day he woke up fine, though his fever continued. He seemed to sleep well enough throughout the day, but then at night, the screaming started again.

We felt we couldn't take it one more minute. We finally got him to sleep once more and then went into the family room to try to figure it out. We asked the first question, "What's really going on here?" The right answer turned out to be, "Joe's sick; he's got a fever." Well, we knew that already. What else? "He hasn't eaten anything all day long." My natural motherly resistance kicked in—"If a kid is sick and doesn't want to eat," I argued, "why should you force him to eat?" My husband wisely helped me past my resistance by simply asking, "Well, is there anything else?" We went through more and more possibilities and finally came up with peace on this simple answer: "Joe's got low blood sugar." We knew something about that already because Joe would get cranky and shaky if he missed meals. What should we do about this? The answer was obvious and we both got a clear StillPoint on it: "Make sure he gets something to eat, even when he's sick." Once we took care of that, we had no more night terrors, even though Joe had given us many traumatic nights with it up till then.

Teenagers and Beyond

Dealing with teenagers and older children at home can be just as complex as taking care of little babies. When you look at them, you think that your almost-grown-up kids are nearly adults, but most of the time you can see that they're really just kids. Indeed, as we've watched our children grow up, we see that they've got lots of maturing to do right up through their twenties. But you can't manage these big kids the way you did when they're little; they're different creatures now. Somehow it's easier to lose it and blow up when they act out. StillPoint can be your absolute ally when this threatens.

We've had teenagers—and beyond—in the house for almost twenty years now. Even so, every new situation gives us another chance to practice patience and find StillPoint. Halfway through the summer, our 26-year-old called up in the middle of the day. It was vacation and my husband was out while I was taking a nap—a schoolteacher's perk on a hot summer's day. Our ten-year-old tapped on the door.

"I'm sorry to wake you," he murmured. "It's Sam. He's sorry to wake you too but he's on the phone and he says I definitely have to wake you up."

I took the call, my heart in my throat. Sam had just taken off to do some job hunting. He'd come home to live after job-hopping for several years, not in college. He came home to regroup and completed an excellent semester, but he hadn't worked during school and had done nothing since, and his empty pockets and my reluctance to fill them required that he get himself a job. He had taken the family car job hunting, so if he was calling, it had to be something bad.

"Mom, I'm sorry I never told you, but I had a speeding ticket last March," he said. "And I just got arrested. There was a warrant out for my arrest. I'm here in the city jail."

My first response was to take him to task right then, but I held back for a moment and thought. Sam had been away for years since high school, working, doing a little school, and messing around. He finally swallowed his pride and came back home, doing a 4.0 semester at our local college. True, we were unhappy with him when he didn't work all summer long, but we were glad he was finally getting himself back on track. I swallowed my harsh words for Sam and said, "You want us to come and get you, I guess."

"I just hate to ask you," he said, "Because bail is a hundred bucks. I know you don't have a lot of money right now," he continued. "I don't really know what to do."

Hanging in the air was the obvious: he had frittered away the summer without getting a job, even though we'd pushed him to do so. Quickly I went through some options in my mind: Leave him in jail for a while and let him learn his lesson; make him promise to pay me back if I bail him out; nag him about employment then and there; call my husband and let *him* deal with the problem. I finally got peace and stillness on the following: Just go get him and you'll know what to do next.

"Okay, son, we'll be there soon as we can." As it turned out, the bondswoman had just gone to lunch and didn't show up for a while, so Sam experienced a few unpleasant hours sitting in a smelly jail cell without any comforts at all, "not even a cushion on the bench!" he declared.

When he walked out of the jail, I didn't say a word, just gave him a good hug. My husband Russell had found us, and when Sam got into the car, Russ simply said, "Well, I won't ask you how your day is going." Sam almost burst into tears at that. We drove in silence for a while and, in a moment of quiet awareness, I asked Russell to drop me off at home. Together they went to pick up the other vehicle and had some quiet man-to-man talk. When they got home, Sam came in to speak to me.

"Mom, I've already told Dad this but I want to say it to you. I think that this is like a wake-up call for me. I've screwed up pretty badly and I'm sorry. Well, I'll go ahead and get a job now even if it's something dumb like at the pizza parlor or something. I'm going to pay you back for the bail and getting the car out. I'm sorry it took me so long to figure this out." He was very embarrassed but he stayed with it. "I'm going to do better from now on." Sam was true to his word and spent the next couple of days beating the bushes till he got himself a job doing janitorial work at a car dealership. He gave us half his paycheck every two weeks till he paid off the debt. Evidently this really was a wake-up call, because Sam continued to work hard and take care of his obligations from that day on.

StillPoint can help you through those everyday moments of panic when young people don't come home when they're supposed to. One night Sarah, at sixteen, didn't make her weekday curfew, eleven o'clock, and didn't show up at midnight, one, two . . . We were getting more than a little upset, then very worried. Sarah was normally punctual and reliable. What could have gone wrong? She was a new driver and we spent a few moments distressed about the family car. Then, as the hours dragged by, we got *more* distressed about what might have happened to Sarah. We started going through all the possibilities in our minds and finally got StillPoint. "She fell asleep!" we realized. "She fell asleep at her friend's house. She'll be home any minute now."

Sure enough, within ten minutes or so we heard the car drive up and Sarah stealthily try to come in through the back door. We were sitting quietly on the living room couch, waiting for her.

"Mom, Dad, I'm sorry I blew it. We were watching videos and I fell asleep."

"Well, go to bed now and we'll talk about it in the morning," we said.

The next day, after a good night's sleep, we all sat down to talk. Before we could even get started, though, Sarah began. "I know I screwed up," she said. "so don't get all mad at me. I missed my curfew. So what do you think about this: I won't use the car for the next week and that'll be my punishment."

That was what we had had in mind anyhow, so we agreed. And from that day on, Sarah has (mostly) continued to be reliable and punctual, and we've tried to access what's going on with StillPoint before we spend half the night sick with worry.

Sometimes you can get a clear answer in StillPoint but you may not understand what it's about. Ericka was just beginning to drive, and she and her sister asked permission to drive four hours to a state basketball tournament. Their best friends were on the team, they said, and they wanted to be there. Russell told her, "I don't know why, but I feel like this is a very good idea."

At first, Ericka wasn't willing to listen because she wanted to go so badly. She packed up the car and took off with her younger sister. About an hour later, they stopped in a small town and called.

"Dad," the girls said. "Most of the time you are so easy with us. You encourage us to try out new things and you give us permission for almost everything. We don't know what problems you feel we could run into, but if you still feel we shouldn't go, we'll come back home."

Russell said, "You're right; I usually let you go. And I still get the feeling this trip isn't for you."

They turned around and drove back home without incident. What would have happened? We never knew because they came back! This is often true about StillPoint; you may feel pretty strongly to do (or not to do) something, but you may not understand all the ramifications. Still, as in the case with Abe choosing to live with his aunt and uncle and go to college, when you heed the message of StillPoint, things usually work out for the best.

When Kids Lie

We don't like to face it, but most kids lie as they grow up—and indeed, many immature adults lie, too, rather than face the music when they "get in trouble." Part of growing up is learning to tell the truth even when it's tough. And when kids lie, it's particularly hard for parents to see through the lie and get to the truth, because we're so emotionally invested in those kids. I remember when one of my teenagers came home roaring drunk. "I haven't been drinking, Mom," she said, "I promise!" And I was willing to believe her, till she puked all over the front walk.

StillPoint is a great resource helping kids grow through the lying stage into more mature honesty. If you suspect a kid is telling a lie, quickly say to yourself, "That's true," and "That's not true." StillPoint will tell you right away what's going on. However, if a kid *is* lying, it's usually unproductive to accuse her of it. We often say things like, "Hmmmm, that doesn't seem to ring true to me," "Are you sure about that?" or "I don't get the feeling that this is the whole truth." Sometimes we use logic: "Let's see then. The only kids home at the time were you and Joe. Are you saying that Joe borrowed your older sister's blouse without permission?"

Once your kids begin to know that you can tell they're lying, it's a first step for them to come clean without any pressure at all. For example, one night Joe came in at curfew and stopped to check in with us.

"I just wanted to tell you," he said. "I wasn't at the party the whole time the way I said. A couple of hours ago, some kids showed up with booze and some of them were using drugs. So my friends and I left. I've spent the last couple of hours at Cam's house, but I'm sorry I didn't call you and tell you," since that was the family rule: if you're not where you said you'd be, you're supposed to call. Joe knew he'd broken the rule but since he was clear and honest with us, that's as far as it went.

When Things are Confusing

When emotions run high and you (or your kids) are highly motivated about something, it can be very, very hard to find peace and stillness as you consider a problem. In our experience, the best way to handle this is to delay making a decision. As an example, Sarah had grown especially tall by the time she was fourteen, and she was beautiful, too. One day, when she was shopping in the mall, a woman stopped her and invited her to attend training to become a model.

You can imagine that this ignited Sarah's imagination—and it spoke generously to her teenage ego, too. She came home with the paperwork to sign up for courses, which were located two hours away in the city. The cost for the seminar was hefty as well, but Sarah was adamant.

We were extremely hesitant about this. The first and most obvious problem we had with it was the huge amount of time and money invested in transportation. We weren't willing to drive to the city and hang around all day every week for several months. The course cost almost a thousand dollars and we weren't sure it was a good investment. No matter how Sarah insisted, there was no guarantee that she'd ever get a modeling job. And if she did, there we were, still obliged to run her four hours round trip to work.

We could see right away, though, that neither Sarah nor we were in an open frame of mind to discuss this. So we used one of our most successful techniques. "Tell us all about it," we said. We gave her a chance to talk through her enthusiasm without any arguments. Then we followed with our winning response, "Give us a chance to think this over and we'll talk again later." Believe me, this can be your lifesaver dealing with kids or in fact in any decision-making. Instead of arguing points back and forth, allow the other person a full communication and then simply say, "Great! Thanks. Give us a little while and we'll talk about it again."

By the time the dust settles, everyone has a chance to think about things and weigh them. When you're calmed down, it's easier to find your StillPoint and get a good answer. In the case of Sarah and her modeling job, we felt sure that it was a terrible idea. But still, we used the following winning technique. This one is so valuable that if you've read this book and only came away with this one skill, it will be priceless for the rest of your life.

What do you do? You validate the person's point of view, 100%, and you keep the discussion positive. Some of the phrases you can use might include:

- "I can really see that."

- "I'd feel the same way."
- "It sounds like a good idea."
- "I can feel that with you."
- "No wonder you feel that way!"
- "Absolutely."

By validating the other person's feelings instead of presenting all your opposing arguments, you leave the discussion open and vibrant, even if you disagree. I like to imagine that this technique keeps the person moving toward you, instead of resisting and moving away. As long as they're in the same camp with you, you can still communicate. Eventually they can step into your point of view without arguing. Here's how this worked with Sarah.

"Well, Mom and Dad, can I take the modeling course?"

"It's really exciting, isn't it? We can only imagine how thrilled you are."

"It's so cool. I can earn $100 an hour once I'm really good at it," she went on, giving us more and more details. Finally she stopped. "But you don't want me to do this, do you?"

"What makes you say that?" we said slyly.

"Well, it means you're gonna have to drive me there every week. And it does cost a lot."

"It sure does." Still in the same camp, agreeing with each other rather than arguing. "And we haven't figured out any good way to pay for it right now."

"And it would mean that I'd have to stop soccer and I wouldn't get to be in the school play," she continued.

"That, too," we said. "So what do you think?"

"You really don't want me to do this, do you?" she said, somewhat sulky.

"Well, we don't. And part of the reason is something you haven't said. We think you are very beautiful, of course, but that's not what we like most about you." Still in the same camp, being positive and not argumentative.

She couldn't resist. "What do you like most about me?"

"You're such an intelligent girl," we went on, "That's what we like so much about you. And we're so proud you made the soccer team. It's hard to see you give that up. But here's the big thing. Sometimes when kids get into modeling, they pay more attention to their image than to the important things, the good nature inside them. We'd hate to see that happen to you, because most of all, we think you're such a good person."

She knew she was finally hearing our argument now, but she had a hard time resisting the positive things we were saying.

"So why don't we all sleep on it for a couple days more?" we suggested, "and then get back together again."

"Ah, never mind. I don't think I'll be able to do this anyhow," Sarah said, disappointed and still a little petulant. We knew though that she'd seen our logic. More to the point, all of us knew that it was going to be a bad choice; StillPoint helped with that. Of course there was no need to rub it in; we let Sarah have her pout, as teenage girls often will, knowing that we'd made our point without having a fight.

If things get out of hand and you *do* end up disagreeing and arguing, we still like to defer till later. I will often say, "OK, we've both had our say. Let's think about this for a while and get back together in a while." Or if one of our kids still wants to fight it out, I say, "I don't think you can hear what I have to say right now. I'll come back and talk later." If there's something I really want and I know very well the other person is not going to agree, I will say, "You don't have to give me an answer now. Just think about it and we'll get together in a day or two." These techniques work with adults as well as with kids. They're great for pain free decision making, because everybody gets a chance to cool down and consider different viewpoints. And that's when they can get peace and stillness on the issue.

Try It

This chapter can save your relationships. If you're willing to:

- say less
- ask the three questions
- then ask the fourth question
- stay positive
- validate the other person
- and be patient . . . .

. . . you can live contentedly in partnership, raise kids more happily, and find your way through hard decisions. You won't have to argue, even when everybody's getting hot under the collar. Most of all, you'll build each other instead of tearing each other down. And most of the time you can end up making the best decisions together, because StillPoint will break you through conflict into peace.

In Conclusion . . .

- The way you see the world—your ViewPoint—creates your reality.
- You can change your ViewPoint—you can change your mind.
- A hierarchal ViewPoint (where someone has to be right and that makes someone else wrong) usually damages relationships.
- You can choose *not* to win!
- Ask the three questions; then ask the fourth question.
- Say less.
- Delay decisions till you're calm and clear.

Chapter Five: StillPoint When You Get Sick

Despite all the TV ads and endless shelves of drugstore offerings, your body wants to keep you well all by itself. It's designed to keep you healthy, even when you're exposed to disease and toxins. Sometimes we may forget that, and it may take a cut finger or a broken bone to remind us that we possess the perfect system—our bodies—for perfect wellness.

You may remember—with some remnant of horror—doing a high school experiment: stroking your finger across the surface of a Petri dish and allowing the bacteria to grow there, then focusing in with a microscope. It amazes us, the microorganisms that flourish all around. Germs are *everywhere* and no amount of disinfectant will ever change that fact, no matter what the ads may say. In fact, disinfecting everything could possibly work against us instead of for us. Some researchers have suggested that certain of the terrible outbreaks of our past, such as the polio epidemic early in the 20th century, resulted in part because we had sanitized our surroundings so much that our bodies no longer had access to everyday germs to gain natural immunity.

With potential infection all around, how do we remain relatively healthy? We do it with our incredible immune systems. As soon as a germ, or poison, or irritant of any kind enters our bodies, whether through breathing, being wounded, or putting our finger in our mouths, our bodies know it immediately, and our immune system sends out macrophages (our first-line-of-defense white blood cells), oxygen-carrying red blood cells, and lymphatic fluid to destroy and neutralize the intruders. In the same instant, our bodies deploy back-up white blood cells that can develop into new macrophages to take over when the first ones self-destruct in defending us.

If we posses such great defenses, then why do we ever get sick? Truth is, as humans, we are much more than just a body system. We are rather a complex synchrony of body, feelings, memories, genetic makeup and constantly changing circumstances. When we're well-rested, properly-fed and generally cheerful, we may escape the flu that's been felling our coworkers, while another time we may go to bed for a week if we've argued with our boss or burned the midnight oil one night too often.

Our immunity is very sensitive, and there are a variety of approaches to building immunity. Most of us know that we should eat well (mostly natural food), drink lots of pure water, rest enough, and exercise, but many of us don't realize that our emotions also have a great deal to do with healthy immune systems. Some years ago, researchers conducted a study showing that negative emotions could dramatically reduce white blood cell activity. They pointed out that if you internalize a negative remark or situation, your immunity might plummet 80% almost immediately. Of course we can recover our immunity by regaining our emotional balance, but it's also easy to understand that negativity and stress might be putting a huge burden on our immune systems, one that we may not easily overcome if we continue the harmful emotional patterns. And if we have persisted in those patterns for a number of years—even without knowing it, even if they're typical stress patterns for our families—we can continue the drain and stress on our immune systems.

After years of working with clients and observing my own patterns of illness—and my family's—I've concluded that just about every physical condition has an emotional component or contributing pattern. Let me point out that this is *not* an absolute, because the exceptions always prove the rule, and in the same breath assure you that this is not a reason to beat ourselves up with guilt. In other words, don't blame yourself when you get sick (another potential source of unnecessary stress leading to guess what? Possibly more sickness) nor should we point the finger at others when they're not well. Instead, understanding that illness has an emotional or spiritual component can help us figure out what we need to do to get well.

You'll understand this right away if you think back to the last couple of times that you were sick. For me, my last head cold followed a big project I had recently finished at school. A local business had donated several guitars to our detention center and we combined these with instruments we owned to teach our very enthusiastic charges some basic chords and songs. I spent a couple of hours a day, for a week, with roomfuls of animated teenagers all armed with guitars. At the end of the week, moderately successful but exhausted, with slightly out of tune strumming still ringing in my ears, I came down with a cold and spent most of the weekend sleeping it off. Just about every time I feel under the weather, I can look at the preceding week or so and notice that I've been staying up too late, eating unwisely, and pushing my limits. Fortunately, much of the time, just sleeping for several hours will be enough to restore my immune system and get me back on my feet.

There are a few books, such as Louise Hays' *You Can Heal Your Life,* that actually link various physical ailments with particular emotional problems. You might find it fascinating to browse through such books to get a notion of how people might associate the patterns of our feelings with sickness. In reality, *knowing* that there's a link is probably less helpful than finding out what you can *do* about it, and for most people, that will be quite individual. And that's where StillPoint comes in.

For example, Suzanne came in for a session complaining of hay fever. Every spring she became thoroughly miserable with itchy eyes, runny nose and a clogged respiratory system. I worked on her feet first, pressing the reflexology zones, and noticed that sure enough, her pressure points were tender in the bronchial area, sinuses and chest. She was also tight in the upper back and neck, very typical for most of us moderns.

Suzanne and I talked back and forth about diet, stress, remedies, all the usual things that we look for when we're figuring out causes. I worked on her quietly for a while through the CranioSacral protocol. Suddenly Suzanne went into a deep and profound StillPoint. We hung there for a while, saying nothing, then I asked, "What's on your mind?"

"I'm remembering the first time I ever had hay fever."

Well, right to the point. "When was that?" I asked.

"It was on a hayride, the first time I met my husband."

More silence.

"Not even during hay fever season," she continued. "It was fall. Out of the blue I started sneezing and running at the eyes. And I've had it every spring and summer since."

Again, silence for a while.

"No wonder," Suzanne mused.

"No wonder what?" I prompted.

"Well, I never feel I can really speak my mind when I'm around Jim," she said. "I'm always worried he's going to find fault with me. He does it all the time."

"He did that on the hayride?" I asked.

"No, not really, but he did tease me then. I think I must have known somehow that it was going to be like that."

"Like what?"

"You know, like I could never have a point of view anymore. Oh, it makes me so mad!" Suzanne grew rigid all over her body as she recalled instance after instance of feeling shamed and silenced during her long marriage. I just kept holding places of tension in her body as she raged and cried—and the tensions one by one released. Finally she quieted down and said, "And I've always known I'm allergic to milk. That could be part of the problem."

StillPoint on that.

"And anyway, I've decided that I don't care anymore. If Jim doesn't like what I have to say, he doesn't have to be around me. I'm fine on my own."

StillPoint on that, too.

We didn't talk after that, just finished the session with Suzanne breathing deeply and quietly, almost asleep. She left the session rested and relaxed. I didn't hear from her for a while—no more appointments or phone calls. Then, some months later, I ran into her at the mall.

"So how's the hay fever?" I asked.

"Oh, I don't have it much anymore. There was a lot of pollen this spring but I only sneezed once or twice. I think I'm pretty much through it."

We chatted about family for a while and went our separate ways. In Suzanne's case, as with so many others, when we finally touched on the cause of the problem and took care of it, the healing takes place so naturally and effortlessly that we almost don't see it coming.

Sometimes it's much simpler than that. As with the case of Ron and his diverticulitis in Chapter Two, our bodies can communicate very clearly with us if we give ourselves the quiet time and space to hear what they have to say. For example, Shauna had been suffering with pains down her left arm for weeks. She was really afraid that she was having a heart attack, but her heart seemed to be just fine. The pain was getting so bad that she couldn't type easily at work. Finally Shauna took a walk by herself in the early evening dusk, watching the farm animals, the trees, the growing gardens. Suddenly she paused in her step and went into StillPoint. "I've got a bone out in my back," she said to herself. "That's what it is!"

The next afternoon she went to the chiropractor and pointed out exactly where the pain was. It took the doctor several moves to correct the malpositioning of the different bones involved, but when he finished his treatment, Shauna's arm pain vanished and stayed away. She did notice, though, that she felt better and better when she took personal time for a walk each day, so most days she adapted her schedule to allow herself that gift.

Always remember that our bodies were created to be well. Our muscles, our nervous systems, our immune systems—everything about us—were designed to support us in health and happiness. There are a lot of people in the world who would like to sell us stuff to keep us healthy. Sometimes we may need some of their products. However, in the long run, our bodies want to keep us healthy. It's in their best interest, after all! We can help them along by listening carefully to our own inherent wisdom and following it with sensitivity.

One of the most important things we must remember is that we are all *individuals* and therefore there's no one cure that is going to help all of us all the time. We can go to the health food store and listen to the sales people recommend all the remedies we absolutely need. But usually, we don't require *all* those remedies, even if sometimes we might need some. We can choose wisely if we train ourselves to check things out with StillPoint.

For instance, Tom had been coming down with frequent infections in the last few months, even though he had formerly been able to fight off colds and flu easily in the past. The only thing that had changed in his life was getting a new girlfriend, and that was all to the good, so far as he was concerned. He and Patty seemed to get along perfectly and enjoyed each other's company a great deal. So what was the problem? Days and weeks dragged along with little improvement, although Tom tried all the cold remedies and vitamins recommended to him. Finally, lying in bed one day, down with yet another cold, an answer popped into his head and he felt a powerful StillPoint.

"It's onions."

Onions?

Yes. Tom had always enjoyed eating lots of onions in his food, but one day, when Patty mentioned that she didn't care for the smell on his breath, he'd cut way back on them. Tom remembered that any time he felt he was coming down with a cold, he always craved raw onions. This makes perfect sense when we remember that onions (and garlic) have been clinically proven to eradicate pathogens—bacteria and viruses alike.

So Tom had a problem, or so he thought, since his heart's true love didn't like the way he smelled when he ate onions, yet they seemed to be the factor that kept him healthy. Still, next time they were together, he took his courage in both hands and told Patty the whole story.

She listened quietly and then said easily, "Oh, don't worry about it. Go ahead and eat onions; it really doesn't bother me that much. I'll just eat onions with you."

Tom had expected much worse! When he resumed eating onions as usual, he bounced back to health—a simple solution to a real problem.

This is not to say that every solution is simple or cheap. Longstanding, difficult problems usually call for big life changes, and often we drag our feet to make such changes. Indeed, when we bring ourselves to the moment of really understanding what we need to do for ourselves, it's often the very thing that we don't want to do and we resist it as much as we can.

For a simple example, Geri *knew* that she shouldn't eat sugar, because it contributed to her yeast infections, made her gain weight, and caused her to feel tired all the time. She knew all of this for a fact and she had experienced plenty of moments of StillPoint on it. Making herself stop eating sugar was another story, however. Like most of us, Geri struggled with her fatal attraction to sugar most of her life. The times she got herself off the seductive white crystals were the times she felt the best. Knowing what we have to do is one thing; actually doing can often be quite another.

Further, when we have poor health, we shouldn't interpret it as being our *fault*. Jane always hated it when people would talk about the connection between mind and body, feeling that people implied that we bring our illnesses on ourselves. Her mom had died of cancer very young, when Jane was only twelve. Their family had lived in Nevada, not far from the nuclear testing during the 1950's, and Jane's family had been identified as "downwinders." Jane's mom, a positive, delightful woman, had died because she was afflicted with others' madness, not her own. And even when our illness does come about from disturbances in our lives at present, this isn't a blame game. StillPoint can help us understand and fix our troubles, but guilt and blame won't help us get better—only improving our lives will do that.

Are the answers always so simple, then, as the examples here? Not always—but often. Even if we have a complex situation to deal with, the first step, then the next and then the *next*, is usually clear and doable, if we're willing. As an example, Keenan, a young man in his twenties, came for an appointment one day. He was having trouble getting to sleep, he said. When he closed his eyes, he felt dizzy and kept seeing quick images zip past his vision. Working with his body, I felt that Keenan was basically a healthy young person. I couldn't pinpoint anything that might be causing the trouble. He mentioned that he had had slightly learning disabilities in school, but that didn't seem to be the problem. Finally, following a hunch, I asked Keenan what he was doing for work.

"I work for an airline," he said. "I book tickets for people who call in."

"Are you working with computers?"

"Uh-huh. I scroll through all the possible flights and book people's tickets."

Of course! He was spending eight hours a day watching a scrolling computer screen. When he got home, he said, he liked to play computer games till bedtime. StillPoint—the constant movement on the computers was causing this problem.

But Keenan wasn't about to switch jobs.

"My family gets free airline tickets because I work there," he said. "I can't change jobs. We'd lose our travel privileges."

The question hung in the air a little while longer as I gave him the rest of his treatment. As he left, he thanked me and I could still see that he wasn't ready to give up this job. Now Keenan knew what the problem was, but he wasn't ready to give up that job. He chose instead to suffer with the problem.

We may think, hearing this story, that the solution was obvious, but Keenan is just like most of us. When it comes right down to the changes that we need to make, we sometimes put up a *lot* of resistance making them.

As a personal example, I feel so much better when I'm exercising every day. During the school year—when I'm teaching and must show up at 8:00 every morning—it doesn't *seem* like a big deal to get up a half hour to work out. We set up a nice exercise space in a pleasant, carpeted, heated garage, complete with music and great equipment, to use during the cold weather. However, when 6:15 rolls around, it's so simple to forget how well I feel when I exercise. It's so much easier to roll over and sleep that extra half hour, even knowing that the exercise will help me more in the long run.

When it comes to really difficult problems, taking the steps, making the changes, can be so much harder. Michelle had known for at least a year that her marriage was over. Her husband Kerry had repeatedly slept with other women, and he was barely civil to her at home. Michelle knew what she had to do: open her own bank account and deposit her own paychecks there; determine if the real estate and car titles were in order; check the family's assets generally; meet with an attorney for initial steps toward a divorce. But Michelle kept putting these things off. Pretty soon she found that she had a hard time getting up in the morning, that she hurt all over. Soon she found herself missing work frequently and ignoring her children. The moment she walked in the door from work, Michelle plopped herself into bed and didn't get up till the next morning—if then.

When she came to see me for the physical pain, Michelle was quiet and unresponsive. As we worked through her body, she kept going into a profound StillPoint, although we didn't talk about it at first. Finally I couldn't stand it any longer.

"What are you thinking about?" I asked her.

"Nothing," she said.

"Hey, it's gotta be something. You're going into StillPoint all the time—like now," I insisted.

"Well . . . I know this can't be it. . . I think I need to file for divorce."

StillPoint on that.

"I just can't seem to get myself up in the morning. I don't even have the energy to get myself to work, much less go through all that effort to file for divorce."

She continued to talk about her exhaustion and bodily pain. I didn't say much till she said, "Oh, I've known for a long time that I need to get a divorce. I just don't know how to get started now."

"Well, what do you think should be the first step?"

Michelle started a long discourse about how vulnerable her children were and how divorce would destroy them emotionally. Finally she stopped.

"Oh, I don't really think that," she said. "I just never wanted to be divorced. My mom and dad divorced and I swore on a stack of Bibles that I would never do that. But Kerry has let me know that he's not going to change. He's just going to keep seeing those other women."

"So. . . what's the first step, do you think?"

"I might as well just go for it. Do you happen to know a good divorce lawyer?"

I didn't know any at the time, but we talked together on how she might find one. We also talked about how straightforward it would be to let the family accountant help her with the finances. I told her about opening her own checking account, which was much easier than she thought. And as usual, after that, I just worked on her body as she relaxed, remained silent, and released much tension. She rose from the table refreshed and quite energetic. As it turned out, Michelle went ahead and took the first steps toward getting her divorce. And, as it often turns out in such situations, everything fell together easily and before she knew it, she was feeling better physically as well.

Exercises

Suppose you find yourself coming down with some ailment. You don't know what it is, but waking up this morning, you've got a headache, you're all congested, and you feel like you weigh a thousand pounds. What do you do?

Ask yourself, **"What's going on here?"**

Let all the possible answers run through your head. "I've got a headache," "I've got the flu," "I'm depressed at work," "This is allergies," "I've got AIDS," anything at all. Allow your imagination to range as you do this. Freely going through suggestions helps release your frustration and tension and can give you a sense of playfulness and openness as you find StillPoint on the situation.

Maybe you find StillPoint on one possibility: "I've got a cold."

Ask yourself: **"What's this about?"** or some similar question.

You'll probably get a clear response right away.

"I'm overtired," "I didn't get enough sleep last week," "I'm stressed out about my daughter," "I talked with that woman who was sick and then I got chilled."

It's always good to know what's happening, because it can give us a clue to the answer to the next question.

Ask yourself: "**What do I need**?"

Again, give yourself enough the go-ahead to take the time to find the right answer. Remember that when we get the right answer, our first response is usually to argue with ourselves and give ourselves every reason we *can't* do that particular thing. If you find yourself in resistance, just remind yourself that it's natural and human to resist. You can always make the choice about what you want to do. Some possible answers? "Stay home and sleep," "Take some vitamins/homeopathic medicines/cold medicine," "Ask my husband to take care of the baby," "Take a hot bath and drink hot lemonade," "Go down to the spa and sweat it out," and many more. When you hit on the right answer, you'll feel StillPoint. Maybe there will be several good answers and you'll know that, too. Now you have the choice of what you want to do. Can you still get yourself up and dressed and go to work? Sure you can, and after you suffer out a long day working, you can come home and take care of yourself. Remember, however, that doing the right thing *first* will always bring the best and quickest results. I always have a hard time recalling that I am not indispensable, that I truly could be replaced for a day or two if needed. This has been a very hard lesson to learn, over and over, but the real lesson has been that I am worth taking the time for. When there's a need, I can take care of myself and get better. Most of the time, sleeping through much of the day will restore my health.

Sometimes, however, the remedy needs to be more dramatic. One year, struggling through those inevitable last two weeks of school, my right shoulder began paining me. I took herbs, homeopathics, hot soaks, massages—nothing would help the pain.

And I couldn't get a clear idea of what to do for myself. Fortunately, my husband knew very well what I needed and I trusted him enough to follow his lead.

"We're going away for a few days," he announced to the family. He directed our oldest daughter to take care of the house, animals, family, and garden (oh, how could I leave all these important things?) and scooped me into the van for a week at a modest resort. It took at least three days for me to even relax into a good sleeping pattern. We ate well, exercised, got a massage, read a lot of books, soaked up the sun, and before I knew it, the shoulder pain had vanished. Further, I felt better all over, and I looked better too. When we arrived home after our little vacation, we found the yard well watered, the animals (and children) in good health, and the house beautifully clean. To be honest, in years past I would have struggled against taking this time, but in the long run, going for a break was exactly what I needed, and I was a better mom because of it, too.

What if you can't seem to get the answer to your dilemma? Work with your spouse, your older kids, your parents, your clergy, a therapist. I believe that we human beings *can* find the answers we need, but sometimes we require a little help to hear them. If you're all alone, you can ask, "What's the first step?" and most times, you'll feel clear direction on what to do.

Dealing with your everyday illnesses—and your family's—is a great way to practice StillPoint. As one pediatrician pointed out, "When there's a problem, I always ask the mother or father what they think. 'It's the left ear,' a parent will say, and sure enough, when I check the child, it *is* the left ear." Trust yourself. Be willing to take that first step. Follow what you find in StillPoint. I guarantee that you'll begin to feel better and better, until you amaze yourself with your excellent health.

In Summary. . . .

- Your immune system is sensitive, and many influences affect your health, including emotions.
- Our bodies can communicate to us—via StillPoint and intuition—what's going on.
- Ask yourself the three questions to help figure out what's going on; then listen in StillPoint to get the answers.

Chapter Six: StillPoint and Chronic Illness

It is difficult to be unwell for a long period of time, and when we are, almost always we may lose sight of what's really going on in our lives as our days fill up with pain and misery. In my experience (and most mind-body practitioners concur) just about every chronic condition has not only a physical aspect but an emotional/spiritual one as well. This can sometimes be hard to accept, because it seems to blame us for making ourselves sick. As a general rule, I don't see it that way, although sometimes we persist in life choices that we *know* are harmful to us and which clearly contribute to our condition. Usually, however, the emotional component of our situation has more to do with unproductive patterns that have shown up in our lives instead of so much being our *fault*. Rather than blaming ourselves for our misery, we can observe our lives—using StillPoint as a measure—and try to understand what might be contributing to our pain.

I'll never forget the most dramatic example of this I've ever seen. A young man came to visit me for a CranioSacral session. Like most of my clients, he scheduled his session in desperation, having tried all the remedies and exercises he could to take care of his problem. Still he continued in terrible pain in his right shoulder, so much so that he could not help with the dishes, drive a car in comfort, or even pick up his six-month-old baby girl.

Just a few years before, Dan had received an honorable discharge from the Marines for medical reasons. He insisted that his extreme shoulder pain was a torn rotator cuff, but no physician, in or out of the military, could confirm that diagnosis. Having heard that CranioSacral therapy could sometimes help in such conditions, he came to see me.

When Dan entered my treatment room, I noticed immediately that he was a pleasant, open, mellow person who seemed to be willing to do whatever it took to get better. He raised his right arm to demonstrate that indeed, he couldn't lift it even so far as shoulder level.

We began our session and although I was willing to treat any problem that showed up, it was just a matter of moments till we were working with the shoulder. I gently manipulated the arm just to the point of pain and held it there. At that time, Dan went into a deep StillPoint.

"What are you thinking about?" I asked.

"Oh, when I was growing up, I had this older brother," he began. "He was never willing to let me win at anything! No matter what game we played, he just had to win. And if I started getting ahead, he'd wrestle me down and pound my shoulder. It made me so mad!"

Dan started to get furious and bellowed out the rest of the story, relating time after time when his brother pinned and pounded him. He began to kick out with his legs and thrash his arms, roaring out his pain. Normally a client hangs back for a few sessions till he gets to know me before he reveals his rage in this way, but Dan was clearly at the end of his rope. He was ready to do whatever it took.

He settled down and then continued the story.

"Then when we were in high school, he was a sophomore and I was a freshman," he said. "We tried out for the basketball team and we both made it. A couple of weeks into the season, the coach cut me, for no reason. I was shooting great and my defense was fantastic, too. My brother, he kept on the team. I tried out the next year and didn't even make first cut but my brother played all season. That was so unfair! I never tried out again even though I was a better player than he was." Dan kept talking, again furious, roaring out his pain, finally breaking into sobs as he recalled his disappointment and rage. When he settled down, he thought for a while and I held the pressure points. He went into a deep StillPoint once again and after a few moments said, "It was when I was in boot camp that this shoulder thing started showing up. It always got worse with each new assignment, especially when my CO was a real asshole." He recalled a few particular instances of injustice when his pain also got quite bad, and then became quiet and peaceful. We finished up the session and he stood.

"Take a look at this," he said, lifting his arm and rotating it in an easy, complete circle. He moved it up and down and all around with complete ease. We were both a little astonished at the improvement. Dan went home a happy man and I only saw him once more, just to check to see how he was doing. He told me he had recalled a number of other instances when he'd been angered by injustice and, working through them, he only continued to improve.

In all honesty, most people require a good deal more time and effort to enjoy such a remarkable healing, but as Dan demonstrated, it can happen. His case reveals the larger truth: when we suffer with a chronic health condition, we can almost always find—with StillPoint—emotional and/or spiritual components that may contribute to our problems.

Is it commonly just one issue, one incident, that can set off our pain? Sometimes it is, but not usually. It is more often a pattern, or set of responses, that can set off our distress.

For example, Mary had always been obedient as a child, both by nature and because she wished to avoid her mother's uproar when she stepped out of line. All through high school and right through college, Mary followed her parents' request that she study to be a registered nurse. Mary never much liked the science courses, especially the anatomy and physiology, but she totally accepted her parents' edict that she become a nurse and continued on to graduate and begin her career.

At one point she began to ache all over and develop a slight fever every afternoon. Pretty soon she had a hard time getting out of bed, making meals, and getting herself to work on time. Her doctor told her she had chronic fatigue syndrome, and although he recommended the usual remedies and approaches for the condition, he could offer her little real help. Before long, Mary was considering going on disability, since she could hardly show up for work at all.

Then one Saturday morning, lying in bed and trying to muster the courage to get up, she started thinking about her life. Going into detail through the major memories of her life, she unexpectedly realized that she had hardly ever made a choice all by herself. She had never opted for anything without considering first off whether her parents would approve, especially her mom. This realization made Mary feel weak, numb and helpless for a few moments, and then she flashed with a rage that she'd never known before. "This is all wrong!" she said to herself. "It's my life, not my mom's!" Instead of allowing herself to feel powerless once more, Mary began to cry and storm aloud at how trivial her life seemed. Nothing she had ever done was what she wanted. It made her so mad!

But what *did* she want? At first blush, Mary hardly even knew, which made her even madder. But deep inside, Mary did know what she wanted. All her life, she'd been wonderful at drawing and sketching. Her most peaceful moments of pure delight had been when she was drawing. Even when she studied for her nursing career, she'd taken her notes with elaborate sketches, some of which were very beautiful.

"What I ought to do," she fumed, "is forget all this nursing crap. I should just become an artist. That'll show them!"

Even in her anger, below the fury, Mary experienced a deep quietness—StillPoint. What did that mean? She could hardly figure it out, but she felt a little bit better and got up and cleaned her apartment, the first time in months.

During the next few weeks, Mary thought again and again about becoming an artist, always returning to that comforting thought as a way of calming down and gaining energy. Finally one day she considered. If even the thought of becoming an artist was so calming and comforting, why not go further? Why not actually do it?

Immediately Mary was seized with guilt for going against her parents' wishes and resistance at even thinking about quitting her good job. Yet as the weeks went past, the thought persisted. Finally, one day driving home after work, Mary thought, "Wait a minute. I am twenty-five years old. I live on my own. I have a good paycheck. I have some money saved up. I'm not a child any more. What's to stop me from becoming an artist?"

On her way home, she stopped at the community college and, overcoming her embarrassment and shame, walked herself right to the registration office, seating herself in an easy chair to glance through the course offerings. As she read through the courses, she experienced a great thrill and peacefulness at the same time. She could do this! She would love this!

But how would she live in the meantime? She realized that with her savings and perhaps a student loan, she could get started. And who knew? She might qualify for a scholarship sometime and even get a government grant, once she was well into the program. On the impulse, Mary went up to the counter and got the registration form.

It would be nice to say that right then and there she enrolled, but she didn't. However, within a couple of months, Mary had arranged her affairs well enough to enroll fulltime in the art program at the college. Everything worked out for her to continue. She adored her studies and excelled, enough to get her desired scholarships, enough to complete the program and graduate as a graphic artist. She found herself a fine job at a magazine company, and it wasn't long till she rose in the business and became a noted and valued artist. Mary was surprised, partway through her coursework, that her fevers and daily pain had vanished. Looking back on her life, as she disengaged from her parents' expectations and followed her own dreams, she realized that learning to make her own choices had much to do with improving her health condition.

When we first consider the possibility that our personal situation might be contributing to our pain, it might seem outrageous, and often we resist the notion, especially when our dysfunction is staring us right in the face. Most of the time, we don't need anybody to tell us what the problem is; we know all too well. We just spend a great deal of energy trying to explain it away or attribute the troubles to something else entirely. When we do this, it compounds our difficulties; not only do we neglect the issues at hand, but we create further conflict inside because after all, we really do know what's going wrong. If we continue to neglect our true selves in this way, our pain often gets worse and worse till we're finally willing to pay attention.

As an example, Gerald had always been a high stress person. He knew it and everybody around him knew it, too. When he was growing up, his mom had always tried to maintain a serene atmosphere at home so Gerald wouldn't be thrown off course, and she had even, for a time, placed in him special-education classes to help clear him from distractions. When Gerald graduated from college, he took a job in computer programming, ideal in many ways because he seemed to have a short fuse dealing with colleagues. However, in recent months, Gerald was finding himself in great pain in his left shoulder and down his arm. His mind flew to the obvious: he was having heart problems. Gerald got more and more upset about this prospect, which only made the problem worse.

Gerald decided to take a vacation to lighten his work stress. He spent a couple of weeks in a beach house, taking his computer with him. To his bewilderment, the pain remained the same or even seemed to get worse as the weeks went on. He returned to work with a good tan but still in a great deal of pain. Finally Gerald gave in and went for a session with a massage therapist to help relieve his problems. None of her ministrations seemed to make any difference, though. "Just as I expected," thought Gerald. "These damn therapists are just a bunch of crock." Just before he left, however, the therapist asked him, "Gerald, is there any time that your pain seems to get worse?"

"Naw, it's always just about the same," muttered Gerald as he pulled on his shoes and socks.

"Any time it gets better?"

"Well, I always feel better right when I wake up in the morning. And sometimes I feel better on the weekends, especially if I haven't done any work."

"Are you left-handed or right-handed, Gerald?" she persisted.

Gerald found himself getting seriously annoyed, but answered curtly, "I'm a leftie."

"You might want to consider that using your computer mouse is contributing to this problem," she said.

At first Gerald wanted to respond, "What a nutcase *you* are," but something inside him agreed, yes, it was the muscles related to using his computer. He felt right, calm, still. "I'll look into it," he said and left.

Over the next week, Gerald experimented with different positions for using the mouse, but nothing seemed to work. Finally he noticed that the pain was greatly diminished when he hung his hands down at his side. Working on that idea, he went home and built himself a little mouse stand to use low by his side, slanted just so that he could leave his arm relaxed and extended.

Sure enough, over the next few weeks, his left-shoulder pain had greatly faded, but it still nagged him sometimes, especially when he had a deadline hanging over his head. Little by little Gerald began to understand that his muscle tightness got really bad when he felt stressed. Although he had a lot of work to do to overcome a lifetime of pessimism and anxiety, Gerald took small steps to overcome his natural tendencies to negativity and began to take things more in stride. Sure enough, his muscle pain grew less and less, till finally he hardly noticed it any more. To his surprise, he also met a woman whose company he actually enjoyed, and before long, Gerald was having a pretty good time in his life. He kept on using his custom mouse stand, and soon he almost forgot the years'-long pain he had suffered in his left arm and shoulder.

Going Deeper

Sometimes the problems can *really* worsen till we pay attention. A longtime friend, Carly, shared this story. She had grown up surrounded by bitterness and criticism. Her father would never acknowledge that she *ever* did anything right. No matter that he treated all members of the family the same; for Carly, it was powerful and it was personal. It all seemed worse because her older brothers responded to Dad's criticism by over-achieving. Not Carly. She dropped out of high school when she was just a sophomore, turning to drugs and drinking and living on the street. She remained away from home when her parents finally divorced, and when she thought about it, she felt that this rift was probably her fault, anyway. Anytime she attempted getting off drugs and putting her life in order, she quickly backslid into the same behavior or worse, including experimenting with harmful drugs with potential for long-term damage.

Later, turning 21, Carly decided that it was time to take her life in her hands and turn things around. At great personal cost, she got herself clean of all drugs, even the prescriptions that the neighborhood neurologist had over-prescribed for her. She moved in with her mother and undertook to get her GED. Then, just a week into the new study program, Carly was making a left turn at an intersection and was side-swiped by another vehicle. She was not badly hurt, but she banged her head and neck painfully. She spent several months recuperating and then figured she'd better get herself back into school again. She passed two sections of the GED with flying colors and then, hiking one day with friends, slipped on the path and slid down the mountain, banging her head once more and further injuring her neck and spine. She was laid up for another few months, recuperating.

Discussing this with her therapist, Carly said, "No matter what I do, I fail. Whenever somebody wants to talk to me, I think they're going to be mad at me. I don't think I'm smart enough to pass the GED anyhow."

"Well, how have you been spending the last few months?" her therapist asked.

"Getting better," she replied promptly.

"Really," the therapist went on. "You mean you don't go anywhere, that you stay home, and do nothing?"

"Well, no, I go out with friends a lot," admitted Carly. "Actually, *quite* a lot. But you know I've had these accidents so I can't work and I think it's damaged my ability to learn, plus the fact I took all those drugs. . . ."

The therapist let those words hang on the air, allowing Carly to hear how hollow they really sounded. Carly began to grin in embarrassment, then stopped.

"You're not saying that I had these accidents on purpose," she demanded, "so I wouldn't have to get on with my life, are you? Those were real *accidents*!"

"I didn't say that at all," smiled the therapist, "but you just did."

Slowly over the next weeks and months, Carly began to notice that she did indeed put herself at risk just when she was getting ready to succeed. She missed an important job interview because she did not want to change an appointment with the dentist in a nearby city. Another time, she drove two hundred miles to see a friend and came home with a stiff back and intense neck pain, which prevented her taking the next section of the GED. Finally she said, "I just keep shooting myself in the foot every time I get close to doing well."

Her therapist agreed. "Everybody does this," she encouraged. "It's just part of life. Now you need to decide to move forward even when it's uncomfortable."

Carly agreed. She determined that she'd cut down on her pain medication, get to bed at a reasonable hour during the week, visit Job Service twice weekly till she was properly employed, and finish the GED. Anytime she noticed she was "shooting herself in the foot," Carly stopped and reevaluated what was going on. Interestingly, she suffered no more accidents, and little by little her back and neck pain improved as the months went by. As with most of us, Carly's recovery took a good deal of time, but every time she passed a hurdle—like the triumphant day when she aced the last section of the GED—she felt stronger and better and more pain free.

If we look closely enough, then, we can see that often there *is* an emotional and spiritual component to our ailments, and again, while it is relatively easy to identify it in many cases, knowing what to do about it and then being willing to follow through can be difficult. When we finally identify it, the first thing we do is dismiss it, try to explain it away, or collapse emotionally and thus fail to deal with it. Why is it that we resist the very thing that's in our best interest? Part of the answer lies in where these problems often originate—when we are very young, when we believe totally in the lessons of our experiences, especially from our parents.

As an example, Julia came to see me because of serious and recurrent stomach problems. She hardly had an appetite and could not digest her food without pain. I had known Julia a long time in the intellectual realm, since she was a noted and devoted feminist author. As we worked, Julia would consistently "translate" our discoveries into something she could explain intellectually; that was her way of manifesting her natural resistance—explaining and quantifying and intellectualizing. As we worked, Julia went into StillPoint and began recalling an early memory.

Julia, six years old, was sitting at her mother's knee as she rocked the latest baby (Julia was fifth in a family of ten children, mostly girls). The mother was discussing some subject with an older sibling, who was demonstrating the worst kind of thick-headedness about it.

Julia tapped her mother on the knee. "Mama, I know a good solution for that," she suggested.

The mother hugged and kissed the baby on her lap, leaned over and brushed Julia's hand away, and continued the discussion with the older sister. Julia remembers feeling ugly, awkward, unwanted, unheard.

"But isn't that always the way," Julia said to me, "in our society! People never listen to the women, even when we have good ideas. A patriarchal society will always negate the feminine voice of reason."

I had to agree with her, although it seemed clear to me that Julia's personal pain was at issue here, not the history of feminism. As we worked, Julia continued this counterproductive pattern of accessing real and painful memories and then translating them into less painful, intellectually correct commentaries.

Julia came back and saw me for many weeks, but we made little progress. With Julia, as with most of us, StillPoint led the way, but she was unable to deal with the very real pain that came with the realizations. We parted ways not long after that, but some years later, I ran into her and asked how she was doing. She had gone through a painful divorce and some financial setbacks, but she was feeling a little better.

"You know, I realized something a while ago," she said. "My mom was a smart woman. And look at my sisters: lawyers, doctors, professors. My mom did a good job. She suffered intellectually as much as any woman in her generation. She had *no* voice. I don't think she was so mean to me, really." It took Julia her own time and her own way to get through her troubles, but she eventually did it.

When we're willing to go a little deeper and access some of the underlying experiences that have created our realities, it is important to find a way to look at them with some kind of distance. I sometimes suggest that people examine these painful episodes as if they were a story: "Once upon a time there was a little girl named
Julia. . . ." you might begin. In this way you can see your story somewhat more objectively and perhaps perceive it in the general context of human pain generally. One of the things that keeps us trapped is that shameful feeling that our situation is particularly degrading or embarrassing or special in some way, when in truth, there are many people who share our kind of distress.

Getting the Help We Need

Julia needed the time to get to her healing in her own way, and often we do. However, sometimes we need a little help to get through. This is particularly true for people who live in a society that supports authoritarian rule, such as religious communities, military families, or other situations where growing up, you felt you could not express yourself. You may not live in that environment *now* but if you grew up in it, you may need some support and help to get through. In my experience, many, many women go through life never expressing their real feelings, and lots of men, too. This may be because our parents still maintained the patriarchal rule of a generation or two ago; it may be simply because our families never learned to communicate well. Who knows? At any rate, sometimes we need help to get through. A good psychotherapist can be a godsend. I know that we may want to avoid the stigma of seeing a "shrink," but I like to see it another way: as finding someone who can truly listen, truly hear us, and give us other ways to look at our life. If you're lucky enough to have skilled clergy to turn to, that's another good option. And if you are fortunate enough to live in an area where you can discover a trusted CranioSacral therapist, you may be able to move forward very quickly, especially since you understand StillPoint from working through this book.

There was a man who came to see me for an embarrassing problem. He experienced extreme pain after sex and indeed could only have sex perhaps once a week without intense discomfort. He described the pain as sharp and cutting and felt it was related to the urinary tract. He also felt that he suffered from frequent urinary infections, though these were not usually diagnosed. He had visited many other therapists of different kinds but to no avail. He had heard that I could help with difficult situations, so in he came.

As we talked, I could see that he had certainly visited many therapists. He knew the jargon and that had become part of his resistance. Finally, as I had my hands above and below his stomach (the chakra point often associated with one's sense of self), he went into a deep StillPoint and stayed there for a while.

"What are you thinking about?" I asked, as always.

"I'm thinking about my dad," he said.

"What about your dad?"

"You know, my mom made him sleep in the spare bedroom almost all his life. This happened when I was just twelve or so. I never really understood why, but I think he did something bad that made her kick him out."

"I wonder," I said lightly.

"Well, we kids really did know. He had an affair with the lady down the street. It was just for a couple of months, but when my mom found out, it changed everything. She wouldn't divorce him, because of the kids, you understand, but she would never sleep with him again. I am pretty sure he turned to masturbation."

"Uh-huh," I said.

He was quiet for a while. "My brother and I masturbated a lot when we were young," he said. It seemed like he was waiting for a negative reaction from me.

"And?" I replied.

"Well, we felt pretty guilty about it. I know for me, I did it all the time."

"And?"

"And what? What am I supposed to say? It's wrong, isn't it?"

"Well, I think it's pretty universal," I said. "People may feel uncomfortable about it, but I think it's natural human behavior, especially for kids growing up."

"So you think it's wrong for adults?" he challenged, somewhat confrontational.

"Does it matter what I think?" I responded.

Silence for a few moments. "No, no, I see your point," he said. "But do you?"

"I guess the most important question is whether *you* think it's wrong," I said.

"Well, our church says it's wrong. My mom always said it's wrong. I guess it *is* wrong. But I have the best orgasms when I masturbate." He stopped for a minute, embarrassed. I just sat quietly and held the StillPoint. "And you know my wife doesn't want sex that often anyhow," he said. "I just get this terrible pain when I do it."

"So for you, it's wrong?" I continued.

He thought for a moment and said, "No, I don't think it's wrong."

I said, "Checking with your body, that feels true." He had remained in a deep StillPoint. "So I guess what we need to do here is let your body know that sex is good and that masturbation is all right for you, too."

He got pretty agitated at this point, not speaking, but clearly struggling with the issue. He seemed a little annoyed that I wouldn't argue the point with him, so he had to have it out with himself, instead. I just waited, holding the stomach area, till he reached StillPoint once more. He began to relax and breathe more quietly, then deeply. Then he started to smile.

"So how are you doing?" I asked.

"I feel like I could just float right out of my body," he said. "I am so happy. I get it. I feel so sorry for my dad. But I totally get it; sex is good. Sex is just fine," he said quietly. "And you know, now I am thinking about something else. I have this great carpenter's shop out behind the garage and I like to build furniture in my spare time. You know, really nice stuff, classy stuff, chairs, tables," he mused. "I haven't done it for a couple of years now. But I'm going to go out there and build something, I think."

"I can see that," I said. "For me, being creative and being sexual seem to be alike—both from my passion."

"Yeah," he said. "I get that. OK. That's what I'm going to do."

I finished the session with gentle CranioSacral work on his head. He lay quiet on the table for some time, then happily got up, paid me, and took off for home. I never saw him again. I hope that his pain went away, of course, and I *also* hope that he moved more and more into the creative/sexual joy that he had begun to access.

Using the Arts to Help Heal Chronic Illness

Even if we don't choose a therapist right now, we can find ways to help us access the emotional components of our situation. I often suggest to my clients that they try some kind of art for this. There are a number of things that work well.

As an example, Mary came to see me for general malaise and lack of energy. She told me she felt very lonely, although married and the mother of six or seven children, all still at home. When we worked, her throat chakra (which often relates to speaking the truth inside us) seemed almost without energy, and she acknowledged that she often had sore throats, sometimes to the point of laryngitis. Whenever we came to a StillPoint, Mary almost invariably had *no* idea of what was going on inside herself. I usually try to avoid suggesting or telling people what I think is the issue, since it brings about reliance on me as a therapist and anyway usually fails to help. Even after two or three sessions, Mary still could never express any ideas or feelings about what she was experiencing when in StillPoint. I believed her. I don't think she really could get it, because she seemed to have bought into a pattern where nothing she said mattered—again, very typical for lots of women, especially those who have chosen wife- and motherhood in traditional family settings. (Please don't think I'm against traditional families here; I'm not! I live in a wonderful traditional marriage with plenty of kids. It's just that many women in such marriages continue a negative pattern in their lives.)

Finally one afternoon, I asked her, "Mary, do you like to sing?"

"Oh, yes, I really like to sing," she said. "I sing in the choir at church."

"Do you sing at home much?"

"No, not really."

"OK, here's my thought. I know you've started going on walks in the mornings after the kids have gone to school. So when you're walking, why don't you try singing?"

"Oh, I could do that," she said.

"And one more thing. When you're singing, don't use the words to songs you already know. It's okay if you want to use tunes that you know, but see if you can make up some words as you go along."

"Oh, I'm not very creative," she said. "I don't think I know how to write songs."

"No, sorry, I don't mean write them. I mean like this: 'I've got the dishes to do, hey now, and there's that letter to write to Mom, don't you know . . ." I improvised, using a familiar tune.

She burst out laughing. "Yeah, I can do that," she said.

Next time she came to see me, I saw that something had changed. She didn't lie down at first, but sat up and looked straight in my eyes, something she rarely did.

"You know, I am *mad*!" she said.

"Ah?"

"And I'm going to do something about it!"

As we progressed through the session, she started talking about her children, who left big messes for her to clean up and who disobeyed her, and about her husband, who criticized her constantly, never supported her with disciplining the children, and spent long hours away from home, leaving all the responsibility to her. Yes, she was mad and she talked it out during that hour and several others to come. It turned out that the singing had brought it out. She'd started to make up little lines as she walked along, and soon she found herself singing stuff like, "What a bastard you are . . . I never get a chance to do anything I want. . . . I'm sick of this life . . .I wanna run away . . . Forget this shit!" She got madder and madder as she went along. Singing made-up words to familiar tunes got Mary past her natural resistance to hearing what her body was telling her. It allowed her to move past her concept of being "nice" and into what was really troubling her. As Mary discharged her anger, she settled down little by little and found herself able to articulate the problems she was having and begin to find good solutions for them.

Similarly, a couple of years ago I happened on one of the best art approaches for this sort of thing. I use it all the time for myself, my students where I teach at the detention center, and my own kids. It is called Touch Drawing, discovered by Deborah Koff-Chapin. She tells this story: she had been trained in the arts to be dispassionate and true to technique, but she was not satisfied by this approach. In fact, she felt kind of miserable because she always wanted to draw faces, yet her art faculty told her that faces were verboten, crazy, passé. Then one day, she was helping a fellow student clean up a board he was using to make prints, and playfully she used her fingertips to design some shapes on the paper towels, which picked up the ink beneath them. To Deborah, the shapes were powerful and attracted her deepest attention. She realized the shapes had come from a place deeper than technique or training. She experimented with the simple technique of rolling paint onto a board, covering it with a suitable paper, and using the fingers to just draw what comes, often with the eyes closed. You can see the results of her work at www.touchdrawing.com.

What happens when you touch draw is that you go beyond your intellectual sense of a situation or reality into what's really going on deep inside you. In my experience it may take several drawings to start accessing your deeper realities. You just roll an oil-based paint on a drawing board (I cut mine out of that board you put on the walls of shower stalls), using a tool called a brayer to roll it out. A brayer is just a rubber roller you can buy at an art store. Then you place some tissue paper or blank newsprint directly on the rolled-out paint. Use your fingers, fingernails, hands, even arms, to make shapes on the paper. Don't pay too much attention to how it's turning out. When you feel like you've drawn everything you might like on one sheet, peel it off, place it on the floor or a table beside you, roll out the paint again, adding more if needed, and repeat. What happens is that you begin to draw out shapes and forms that may give voice to what's going on inside you. Aside from that, it's a lot of fun. Just keep drawing, peeling off the paper, rolling, and drawing again. You're finished when you feel like you've had enough, but remember, if you find yourself meeting internal resistance, as sometimes happens when you're working with StillPoint, allow yourself to move past the resistance; keep drawing; see what comes up.

You can see some powerful examples of how this works on Deborah's website, and here's one of my own. I got home from work one day feeling restless and unsettled, though I didn't know what was bothering me particularly. I went out to my workspace—a nice artsy corner in our renovated garage—and set up for touch drawing. I found myself making round shapes—a stomach—a pregnant stomach—lots of round, pregnant stomachs. I started wondering what was going on there. Having borne nine kids, I assumed that I probably hadn't dealt with the issues of having grown enormous nine times, a lifetime's worth of pregnancies. Then I found myself drawing a big round stomach with a woman's face peering out. Finished with that, I felt I was done. Later I took out the sequence of drawings to see how I felt. Yes, I was feeling chagrined at weight gain and anger at feeling my life had passed me by while I was childbearing and taking care of multitudinous babies. More than that, however, the face-in-the-womb drawing fascinated me. Yes, that was it. I realized in deep StillPoint that I was in a transitional period of my life, that I was learning profound and key things that were going to birth me into a different person, a new life. Thinking over what this particular year had brought me, I had to recognize that this was a good interpretation of the series of drawings. Things were changing (for the good) and I was uneasy, just as we always are during change. It was great! I liked the womb drawing so much that after it dried, I mounted it and hung it in my office to remind me that great change was on the way.

By the way, it's a good idea to buy water-based oil paints for easier cleanup, although regular oil paints also work. When you're done, just roll the paint over the board for a while and roll the excess onto newspaper or a spare sheet of paper. Let everything dry and put it away. It's best to work in a ventilated space because oil paints smell somewhat strong. It is easy to find the materials you need for touch drawing at an art supply store or even just a discount store like WalMart or Kmart.

However, if you don't have time or resources to put together stuff for touch drawing, you can try a technique I've adapted from Betty Edwards, author of *Drawing on the Right Side of the Brain* and *Drawing from Your Soul.* Just gather some paper and a fairly soft-lead pencil. Seat yourself in a place where you can work quietly for a while and no one will disturb you.

For the first round, fold one paper in thirds both ways so you end up with nine squares when you unfold it. Label each square with an emotion or quality: happiness, excitement, grief, anger, jealousy, femininity, joy, fear, worry, depression, or any others that come to mind. Then in each square, draw the lines and/or shapes that communicate your feeling about each emotion. You just do this by sitting quietly till you know just how to move that pencil to really render your gut response to each word. It's nice to put this paper away for a day or two and then take it out and look at it. Often the lines reveal deep feelings that you might not have been able to express totally in another way.

For the second round, think of a person or situation that you're dealing with. In your mind, call the paper by that name: "my ex-girlfriend," "being fired," "having AIDS"—that sort of thing. Again, sit quietly and wait till you and your pencil seem to know just what kind of line to draw to represent your response to the subject. Draw every line, large or small, that seems to pertain to the subject. It may not turn out to be actual forms or figures that you can recognize, but the lines themselves will reveal and articulate your real feelings about the subject.

When you're done with your picture, turn it over and write its name on the back. You can continue on and do a series of them on different subjects (or more on the same), and then you can move to the next phase. Take some time to really look at your drawing; try to understand it; see if you can feel the feelings that the actual lines evoke. Now turn the paper over (or get a clean sheet) and write about the drawing. What did you learn about your situation or relationship by examining your lines and forms?

I've done this many times myself and used it with troubled youth and with college students. Invariably these drawings reveal aspects our lives that we may not have been aware of. Sometimes we enter a deep StillPoint, as we understand new things, filled with compassion for others. Sometimes the drawings show us where the changes need to be made and help us resolve to do something hard. We may reach new understanding about our relationships, which can give us patience in dealing with difficult realities. Be sure that you do this project somewhere that you can feel safe and uninterrupted. You don't have to show these drawings to anyone; they're for you. But sometimes they turn out so beautiful that you do like to share them with others!

Try It

Most of us struggle with some kind of chronic problem, whether it's a cranky shoulder or a life-challenging disease. Most of the time, our ailments manifest themselves physically and sometimes they are mostly physical, perhaps inherited genetically or otherwise occurring. However, because we're a whole person, our physical disorders often do have an emotional component, perhaps as a root cause, perhaps as the result of having the problem.

Think about the physical problem that's troubling you. Take some quiet time to really think about it. When you do, what sorts of memories, images, or thoughts pop up? Pay attention to those thoughts, one by one. If any of them are significant to dealing with the problem, you can often find StillPoint when you think of them. If you like, write them down. Ask yourself, which one of these might be a first step in dealing with my condition. Most of the time, you'll feel a significant StillPoint on one of them. Then ask yourself, what's the first step for me to deal with this? Morning walks? Visits to a therapist? Vitamins? A conversation with my mom? Music? Once you hit on the right answer, you'll again feel peaceful and still. Even if you feel resistance and anxiety as you approach the subject, tell yourself that you've got what it takes to take the next step. Then do it! You can repeat this process many times as you deal with the problem. With good fortune and persistent work, I believe you'll be able to move toward wholeness and wellness as you use StillPoint to help overcome problems that may have plagued you for years.

In Summary. . . .

- There is often an emotional component to long-term ailments.
- We should never blame ourselves for our illnesses, but seek to understand what's going on.
- Singing and art can bring surprising insights and healing.

Two brothers, now grown up, were reminiscing about their childhood.

"You know, I was always jealous of you," said Bill. "Dad never paid any attention to me. It was always Tom this, Tom that. He never even glanced at me. No matter what I did, it was never good enough. I always wished I could be you."

"You've got to be kidding," Tom said. "Didn't you know? Dad had been—well, he always touched me . . .you know . . .. I've been in therapy for years now trying to deal with it. He even admitted it, but it doesn't take away the harm he did."

Even if we lived in the same house, we've all had a unique experience growing up. And if we're honest, we know that the Leave It to Beaver household, perfect in every way, never really existed. Everybody has suffered in some ways, sometimes very serious ways, as we've moved ourselves into adulthood. That doesn't mean that we need to become the Eternal Victim; rather, the difficult things in our lives can be turned into positives with a little turn of perspective.

Sometimes we think that if we could just revisit to a happier past, things would have been better. But it's not always true. Even when Ozzie and Harriet were raising the perfect family on TV, people struggled and suffered in families and for centuries before. As an example, one of my relatives, Esther, was born near the end of World War II, and her younger sister appeared just a year later. Her parents carried on a never-ending cycle of separations and uneasy reconciliations, complicated by her father's frequent affairs. Being Jewish only made it worse, because it meant a lot of teasing in those days, and Esther looked the part, right down to the nose, she always said. Over the years, business had only gotten worse for her dad, and it seemed like when he got home, he could be counted on to do three things: barely speak to Esther's mother, bring her sister Dina clothes and treats, and beat the hell out of Esther, even throwing chairs sometimes. When Esther was fifteen, she begged her mother to go live at a neighbor's house, to keep her safe. Esther's mother tearfully agreed.

Unfortunately, there was an uncle living in the home who preyed upon Esther, slipping into her alcove and abusing her every night. Esther became pregnant at age sixteen, and for the longest time she could not bear to tell her parents. Meantime, her father finally left her mother for another woman, leaving the mother bitter and dirt-poor. Esther's mom went out to work at a time when women seldom entered the workplace, and Esther returned home, bearing the family shame and ridicule for her condition. She did not dare tell anyone that the uncle had taken advantage of her so everyone assumed that she had been promiscuous. As soon as her pregnancy became apparent, Esther's mother sent her off to a school for girls, where, alone and despondent, Esther gave birth to a baby boy, whom she left at the school to be adopted by some other couple.

Although this seems a dismal story indeed, it may also be very familiar. In Esther's case, most of her life, she continued to play out her pattern of abuse. She married and divorced two alcoholics who kept her captive in verbal and physical cruelty. However, when Esther turned about forty, something changed.
"I don't have to do this anymore," she said. "I'm *not* going to do this anymore." She found herself a Women's Center that offered therapy, to be paid on a sliding scale. Even though she grew up without hope and with every chance of replicating the abuse, Esther moved out of the cycle and into a happier life.

Knowing that we all have suffered some hardship, unkindness, or difficulty in our lives; can we ever get over it? I would say yes, much of the time we can move through the pain into more balance and health. Some things may take years to heal and from some we may never fully recover, but that's the adventure of this life, to keep moving forward and transcending.

Stored Memories

CranioSacral therapy, like other healing methods, teaches that we hold memories in our minds and *also* in our bodies, stored in the cells and tissues. The connection between a physical symptom and an earlier experience may sometimes be easy to recognize, as with Dan who was slugged in the shoulder as a child and whose dysfunctional shoulder came to light when he joined the Army. And sometimes the connections are not so obvious, and we may often know the physical discomfort for a long time without remembering any incident related to it.

In *Waking the Tiger, Healing Trauma,* author Peter Levine asks why wild animals, going through the trauma of kill-or-be-killed every day of their lives, don't end up with post-traumatic stress syndrome or other stress-related diseases. His answer: they release the tension from their bodies by vigorous movement and by making noise (I sometimes use the term *vocalizing* to describe this in people). We humans on the other hand will go through traumas and next freeze up, encapsulating the negative energy someplace in our bodies. Dr John Upledger terms these frozen areas "energy cysts." Locating and releasing this frozen energy can help us get rid of our physical pain and also begin to cut loose our emotional hurts as well.

Locating the painful area in your body is easy enough; it's usually driving you nuts. The next step can be tricky, though: identifying a stored experience or memory relating to the pain. At first blush, most of us can come up right away what it's all about, although we usually immediately put up resistance, denying that the past has anything to do with it. However, once we get past that resistance, like the animals, we often need some vigorous physical movement and often some vocalizing to release the frozen energy from our bodies. And when that's all done, we can come to the first steps of peace about what happened and begin to heal from it.

Jorge came from a home where spanking (which often became beating) was the order of the day. His dad did the beating; Mama stayed in the background and wept. Because of that, Jorge tried hard not to cry when he was being beaten, so as to make things easier on Mama. However, as Jorge grew, he found it more and more difficult to take those beatings passively. At nine or ten, he began kicking his dad when he'd start hitting. His dad would grab his legs and hold them between his knees while he thrashed his son. Finally, like many boys in this situation, when Jorge turned fifteen, he stood up to his dad and slugged him a good one when he tried to beat him. His dad never hit him again and Jorge thought he was done with all of it.

Some years later, however, Jorge found himself struggling with lower back pain as well as with a mean temper of his own. Jorge knew that in his heart he was not a violent man and realized that he was taking on his father's temperament when frustrated. Jorge was planning on getting married the following year and had no intention of repeating the cycle of abuse he had grown up with. He came to see me about his lower back early one fall.

We began our session and I worked for a while on the sacrum and lower back without much result. I will often check the CranioSacral rhythm and the body generally at the feet, holding them gently. As often happens in these sessions, I followed the pattern in the body by holding the feet a little more firmly, then quite firmly indeed.

It sent Jorge into a fury. "Let go of my feet, you bastard!" he hollered.

Well, we were onto something. I loosed my hold on his feet and touched them softly once more, asking, "What's going on, Jorge?"

"Oh, it was my dad," he began, telling me the whole story of the childhood beatings. As he worked into the story, he started moving his legs restlessly. I held the feet a little more firmly and asked, "Is this okay?" to make sure I wasn't pushing him too hard into his issues.

"Yes! Hold them suckers!" he hollered as he pushed against the pressure of my hands. I returned equal pressure, no more, heightening the firmness as much as he gave. Finally he was yelling his anger at his father, swearing at him, calling him every name in the book. In moments, he began crying as he expressed his concern for his mother and his exasperation at being unable to do anything about the whole situation. I stayed with him, loosening my hold on his feet as he sobbed and relaxed. As soon as he was still, I moved to the lower back and worked on the sacrum once more. This time it moved easily and released the tension long stored there.

When we were done, Jorge sat up and swung his legs over the side of the table. He said, "What do you know . . . it feels a lot better. A *lot* better!" he said as he got up and moved around. He sat down on the table and told me the story of how he'd stood up to his dad when he was fifteen, and how his dad never touched him again. "Or my younger brothers," he added. "I made sure of that." Jorge came to see me a couple of times after this, and we spent some useful time working on anger issues. From that first treatment, however, his lower back improved dramatically and stayed relatively pain-free.

Baby Suffering

Dr. David Chamberlain has spent a good part of his career researching the mental states of babies. Instead of being semi-conscious and unable to fully experience pain, as been assumed for so many years, babies seem to be very aware from the moment of their birth—and before, as they are now thought to be conscious in the womb as well. This is nothing new to many prospective parents, who buy music tapes for their babies-in-embryo to listen to and sometimes sing and talk to them as well. It is well established that babies are born with the ability to respond to their parents' voices.

My favorite story about this comes from Dr. Chamberlain's book, *Babies Remember Birth.* A young orchestra conductor and string player opened a new score one day, preparing to present it to his orchestra later that evening. As he read through the score, he discovered that he somehow knew this piece. He knew where the page turns were and he realized he could sight-read it almost flawlessly the first time through. How could he possibly know this music? So far as he knew, he'd never seen it before.

Later that week, during Sunday dinner with his parents, he mentioned the incident to his parents. "Oh, yes," said his mom, a cellist. "I learned that piece when I was carrying you. I played it every day." Evidently the embryonic boy, nestled between his mom and the cello, "learned" the piece along with her.

Sometimes we need to reach clear back to our earliest times to figure out certain problems. Suzanne came to see me for depression and lack of energy. We met for a few weeks with some good results but not much forward progress. Finally, she confided, "I want to tell you something. Not now, of course, but once in a while over the last year, I've wondered what it's like to commit suicide."

Oh, no—a real danger signal if ever I'd heard one. "How often do you think about this?" I asked.

"Oh, not for months now," she said, "but it comes up once in a while."

"Is someone hurting you? Are you . . ."

"Oh, nothing like that. My husband's great and I love my job. It's just weird . . . comes out of nowhere."

I found myself working on the stomach area, which, energetically, is the chakra related to our sense of self. There Suzanne went into a deep StillPoint but couldn't retrieve any particular trauma or memory. Finally I asked her to think back to the first time she'd started thinking about suicide. She remained in StillPoint as we went back: not as a teenager, not a school-child, not as a toddler.

"Oh my gosh!" she said. "You're not going to believe this. I just remembered the funkiest conversation!"

"Great. How old were you, do you think?" I said.

"That's the funky part," she said. "It's when I was born. The doctor was saying, 'It's a girl,' and my mom was out cold and couldn't hear anything but my dad said, 'Oh, darn, I was hoping for a boy,' and the doctor said, 'Well you know we can't put her back,' and they were both laughing about it when they handed me to the nurse, and I thought they weren't going to keep me, but later I guess they brought me to my mom."

We hung out there for a while and I held the StillPoint.

Suzanne spoke again. "I thought they didn't want me," she said. "And there wasn't a thing I could do about it. They couldn't put me back, they said. So I guessed I'd have to die. I've felt this my whole life!" She was talking louder, then yelling. "It's not fair! I was just a little baby!"

She was breathing rapidly, which turned into light sobs. Then she stopped, and her StillPoint held. "It's not true, though," she said quietly. "They wanted me. They were just joking. Hmmmmm. . . ."

She moved out of StillPoint and I finished the treatment, working on her shoulders and head.

As she put her shoes and socks on she said, "Well! That takes care of that!" I knew she meant the suicidal tendencies, and sure enough, although she came back to see me once in a while,

Suzanne's mood improved and remained positive—no more suicidal thoughts.

Is it always that easy? No, but it can be. In my experience, when we're ready to access the source of our pain, our bodies and minds are generally our allies, not our enemies. We are meant to be well; our whole selves tend to wellness. This, however, can extend to the spiritual and moral realm as well, because sometimes our bodies determine that they're not going to permit us to cross moral boundaries anymore.

Try Counting Back

It's very simple to use this technique yourself. So much of the time our negative habits and out-of-proportion reactions to things originate in our childhood. We may feel ashamed about using the bathroom, feeling our sexuality, eating in front of others. We may endure a multitude of phobias, including fear of heights and fear of public speaking. There are countless phobias of all types; I was fascinated one school year to meet a teenager who was terrified of plants and another who was scared of cotton balls. Sometimes we freak out when we hear certain combinations of words. The possibilities are enormous, because these habits, patterns and traumas start off in our childhood experiences. Most of the time we just deal with them the best that we can, but if we want to change them, it's not that hard.

Counting back, as Suzanne did in the previous story, is a simple way to access the beginnings of our troubles. Everything that happened to us is stored in our minds and our bodies. When we pinpoint some pain, habit or emotional state that we don't want anymore, we can find it and clear it.

Here's how you do it. Find a quiet space, even if it's only in your mind. You can actually do this anytime your mind is free, driving a car, doing yard work, or doing the dishes. Think about the thing that's bugging you but you can't quite figure out. Get centered and still identifying it. That's important because sometimes we think something is the problem when it's really something else. For example, Jennie thought that she was afraid of meeting new people so she avoided it as much as she could. In reality, however, Jennie detested being teased. Knowing that, she used this technique to count back and locate the first time she was made fun of. She found the moment—a time when she wet her pants sitting in kindergarten during story time—and cleared it.

Once you definitely identify what the problem is, if you don't immediately realize how it got started, just stay focused and say, "This started when I was an adult," "This started when I was in my teens," "This started as a child," and so on. When you get a StillPoint on the general time period, you can state, "This started when I was ten, nine, six," and so on. As soon as you get StillPoint on the time, stay quiet with the concept that it started at that time and see if you don't begin to remember something about it. In just about every case, people suddenly get it! "Oh, I remember, it's when the softball hit me hard in the stomach!"

If you don't recall a particular incident, that's okay. I always tell my clients—and myself—"You have all the time in the world." During the next few days, think about the thing that you want to clear and the time period it happened. Often it will come to mind, especially when we're relaxing into sleep or performing a repetitive task. When you finally understand what happened, you can use one of the following techniques to clear it. The results can amaze you as you get rid of fear, anger, and bad habits that have plagued you for years.

A Conversation with Your Body

As an example, when she got her last pap smear, Julia had been diagnosed with cervical cancer. It had not progressed very far, but she was devastated. Thirty-two years old, with a fine career, a steady-on marriage and two children, Julia seemed to have everything. This type of cancer didn't run in the family, and she had a basically healthy lifestyle. What could have gone wrong? A longtime friend, she came in for a session one day to try to make some sense of her life turned upside down.

Working on her lower abdomen, we went into StillPoint, not surprisingly. There I used a technique learned from Dr. Upledger: I had Julia ask the area affected, the cervix, what was going on.

"That's kind of weird," Julia said. "How do you talk to a cervix, for God's sake? And how does it answer you?"

"Well, just pretend it's got a personality or something," I said. "You ask it the question and just listen. I'll check for StillPoint. Whenever you go into a StillPoint with an answer that comes up, you can tell me what it was."

"Okey-dokey, I'll try anything," she said lightly. "OK, there, Cervix, you gonna talk to me?"

We waited a second: StillPoint. "What're you thinking?" I asked.

"Oh, that's dumb," she said. "I was thinking, 'I am so mad at you I'm gonna kill you!'"

"No kidding!" I said. "Ask her what about."

"What are you mad about?" Julia said, referring to the cervix. She still thought it was a big joke, but she was willing to play along—for the moment, anyhow, till she got the next answer. "Oh, never mind," she said, blushing bright red, "I don't want to talk about this."

"Okay," I said.

Hardly a minute passed, then she said, "But I guess I'd better. You want to know what the cervix said to me?"

"Sure."

"Well, Cathy, don't think bad of me. You've known me for years; you know I'm not a bad person."

"Yep, I know that," I said.

"Well," said Julia, still faltering and blushing, "My cervix said, 'If you don't stop having your affair, I'm gonna kill you."

"Ah," I said. "So what do you think?"

"You're not mad at me?" Julia said. "You don't think I'm horrible?"

"No, how could I think that? You're my buddy, Julia, I don't think badly of you. But it looks like your cervix does." We laughed.

"No kidding," she said. "I don't know what to do about this."

"Go ahead and ask your body," I prompted.

"OK. So, Cervix, what am I supposed to do about this?" We waited, then StillPoint, then the answer, "'Just stop having the affair and don't do it again. That's all.' That's *all*? My God!" she said. "I've been seeing this guy for almost a year now. In fact, I know him from work. How can I face him? How can I tell my husband?" She remained quiet for a while, and then said, "Oh, I see. I can just do it. I can do this. Maybe my husband won't be able to stay with me; I don't know; I've got to accept that possibility. And I'm going to have to break it off with Bryan. I know this. I can do this."

We said nothing more as we finished the hour, mostly working on feet, shoulders, head. She got ready to go and turned to face me. "I don't know how you feel about this, but it doesn't matter. I'm going to do the right thing."

Long story short: Julia broke off her affair completely and confessed everything to her husband, who was eventually able to deal with it and they stayed together. She decided to quit her job and stay at home for a while. Some months later she went in for a checkup and was stunned to learn that her cervical cancer was in remission. To this day she remains pretty convinced that her cervix had given her a life-or-death ultimatum.

I've used this technique time and time again. It seems simple, almost childish, to have a talk with some part of your body, but some contemporary healers are convinced that every organ, every tissue, every cell, has an innate intelligence on its own at the same time that it functions as part of the whole person. If you're willing to be playful and use your imagination a little, it's not a far stretch to think that you can dialogue with your body and get important information that you need.

When you do try this dialogue, please be aware that you will undoubtedly put up a lot of resistance to the process and to any answers that may come out. In fact, you'll probably feel like a total fool when you first start this. Once you get started, however, you may find the method interesting indeed. For example, Beth came in to see me because she was struggling with menopausal hot flashes. She'd tried hormone therapy, herbal therapy, nutritional therapy and everything else you could think of, with no results. We began our session with the feet as usual and went right to the abdomen. There we hung out in StillPoint for a while with no palpable results, until I suggested that we dialogue with her uterus.

Beth has a great imagination and she was right up for the experience.

"Hey uterus!" she said. "Oh! It doesn't want to be called 'uterus.' It wants to be called Daisy. OK, hey Daisy!'

It was fun seeing Beth play with the idea—until Daisy started having her say. "You are such a waste of time," said Daisy the uterus, via Beth. "You never do a single thing you say you will. Oh yeah, you're gonna get a massage. Oh sure, you're going on vacation. Oh yeah, right, you're spending some money on yourself. Fat chance! Ha! Never in my lifetime!" she said.

"Wow," said Beth, speaking for herself. "She's furious!"

"So you might as well get this," continued Daisy, unabated. "Forget it! I'm not playing! You might as well get used to it! It's hot flashes as long as I can get my fingernails into you."

"My God!" said Beth. "She is totally out of control. What on earth can I do about this?"

Before I could get a word in edgewise, Daisy continued. "You want to know? Well, I'll tell you. Tonight *Ken* does the dishes, not you. You're going out to the movies, *alone*. And tomorrow you're going to take a day off. No, two," said Daisy, warming to her subject, "you're taking two days off and then comes the weekend. I think you're going down to Vegas. You're going to sleep, gamble, swim and eat yourself sick at the buffet. No arguing now," warned Daisy, recognizing the familiar resistance in Beth who was ready to offer all the reasons why she couldn't go. "It's up to you. Do what I say or the hot flashes continue."

"Dang, she's a fair bitch!" said Beth. We both burst out laughing.

"So what do you think?" I asked.

"I think I've got no choice. It's a Las Vegas weekend for me."

It wasn't easy making the change from being an enabling mommy/wife to a woman who took care of herself, but Beth threw herself into it, starting that very weekend. She launched into good self-care confidently, and it wasn't long till I saw her again, shopping at the mall with Ken.

"So how are the hot flashes?" I asked.

"Oh, a thing of the past," she said, arm in arm with her husband and smiling amiably. "We've decided: menopause is a great thing!"

Accidents

You can't always trace everything back to an emotional state or distress. Sometimes longstanding pain can relate to an accident or other physical trauma, even though we may not remember it. We can access it through StillPoint, however, and give our bodies the opportunity to release and clear it.

Just about everybody's suffered their share of bumps on the head, especially growing up. Most of the time we don't think a thing about it but just get up and go on our way. Usually we recover and that's the end of the issue, but not always. Peter had been suffering with intermittent headaches for a couple of years now. He had gotten used to taking pain relievers all the time, but recently, the throbbing had gotten worse. He came in to see me and as we worked, we talked over the usual reasons for headache: dehydration, constipation, food allergies, stress. None of that seemed to apply to Pete. He had always eaten fairly healthy, exercised plenty, drank lots of water, and was rarely constipated. He was copasetic with his job and had good roommates at college and a girlfriend he loved. Everything seemed fine with Peter except the headaches.

"Hmmm," I said. "Do you remember when they first started?"

"Nah, I can't remember," he said. Then we hit StillPoint as I held his head in my hands. "No, wait!" he said. "Yes, I do. How dumb of me to forget that. I had this accident on my motorcycle."

"Hurt bad?" I asked.

"No, not really. It wasn't a bad fall at all. Only I hit the side of my helmet as I fell. Just like the time—oh, I remember! I can't believe I forgot this—just like the time I was hit by the swing at school. You know, those tire swings? I was walking in back of one and my friend swung back and knocked me right on the side of the head."

We remained in StillPoint. "Yup, that seems to be the problem," I said. "Anything else you remember?"

"Well not really, only that there wasn't any grown-up on the playground, so I just got up and walked back to the building. I just sat there in the shade till the bell rang and it was time to go in."

We worked quietly for a while. Usually in a CranioSacral treatment, you can get a fair amount of movement as you work on the head, but Peter's remained quite stuck. I got some results in that session and more and more during the following few weeks. By the time we'd worked once a week for two months, we'd released most of the tension in Peter's head. And not surprisingly, the headaches were mostly gone.

Often when we get hurt, we're too self-conscious to scream and yell, although we may want to. Girls don't want to be embarrassed and guys don't want to look wimpy, so we hold ourselves back when what we really want to do is scream our guts out—just like little babies do, just like dogs and cats will do when they're hurt. But no, we hold back and absorb the pain without a whimper, if we can. That again creates frozen energy inside us and sometimes can create chronic pain. If you can think about the pain and then get in touch with its origin, you can often release it without the help of a therapist. What often happens is this: you may feel like screaming or yelling—as you would have done when you first got hurt, if you could have—and you may also experience a unique physical phenomenon called unwinding. Instead of tensing up and taking the blow as we did originally, our bodies will sometimes turn or twist as they release the physical disturbance that came with the injury. If you can find yourself a safe space to let this happen, say a carpeted spot in your family room or the soft lawn in the back yard (allowing for the possibility of needing to holler some), you can often get rid of some chronic pains.

You can do this by sitting or lying comfortably and putting your hand on the place that hurts. You might experience the memory of the injury as you sit there. If you feel like vocalizing at all—saying ow! or moaning, or crying, or swearing—just do it. If your body wants to rock or turn, give yourself the time and space to do that. Oftentimes you'll get a memory that goes along with the experience, as Jon did when he worked through a chronic leg pain. He suddenly had a flashback of his best friend saying, "Oh don't be a sissy. It didn't hurt that bad." In the memory, Jon just sucked it up and got back on his bike, but as he processed the memory, he allowed himself to say, "Oh, Richard, leave it alone. This hurts! Go on home if you want. I'll be coming later." Then Jon stayed with the pain, rocking and saying, "Ouch!" a few times till he felt the tension move out of his leg and the pain dramatically reduce.

When you're dealing with deeper, more disturbing injuries that affected you both body and spirit, it can sometimes take a little time to get to the core of it. Damage done by physical, sexual or emotional abuse can take some time to heal, and sometimes it may take a good deal of effort all your life to find balance and peace after enduring such abuse.

Whose Point of View?

One of the most powerful approaches I've found in such cases has to do with point of view. It's natural to see things from your own point of view; in fact, how could you see it otherwise? Still, allowing yourself to play with a different point of view, just as we did with dialoging with the body, you can often gain insights that will move you more quickly through your distress.

As an example, Cecelia came in for a session one day. She had been through umpteen therapists, never getting any satisfaction. Her issue? She had been raised by a single mother who had been cold and unloving, unwilling to touch or hug Cecelia, hardly willing to even talk to her. All her life Cecelia had been searching frantically for warmth and acceptance, trying alcohol, drugs, art, sex, and frantic physical activity, even enlisting in the Marines. She'd been through several unhappy lesbian relationships, thinking she was gay because she could not relate to men at all. The problem was, she wasn't relating to women very well either. Like many others who have gone to many therapists, Cecelia was all too familiar with the jargon and very resistant to being "therapied."

We worked for several weeks, and although we would occasionally have a breakthrough, Cecelia seemed to be going nowhere. Finally one day, she was recalling a time when she was imprisoned in a large crib far past the time when she was a baby.

"That is so wrong, that is so abusive!" she ranted. "My mother shut me in this big crib so she wouldn't have to take care of me, so she wouldn't have to hold me!"

"Can you see that in your mind's eye?" I said.

"I sure can! I can hear myself, screaming my guts out."

"And what's your mother doing?"

"She's just sitting there, ignoring me. She's not doing a thing."

"You want to try something?"

"I guess," she said.

"For a moment, try to pretend that you're your mom. Get into her head; try to feel it from her point of view."

"No way," said Cecelia, going into the familiar resistance. "She's such a bitch. I'm never doing one thing for her again."

"OK, you don't have to. But it might be interesting to try this."

After a few moments, Cecelia went into StillPoint and said, "Oh, my God." She lay there quietly for a moment as I held StillPoint at her stomach area. "I don't believe this. My mother was sick; she wasn't well; she was in deep trouble."

"What are you seeing?" I asked.

"She was really depressed and she was all alone. Her mother had kicked her out and she was living all alone in Detroit, far from any relatives. My mom—she had clinical depression—I had no idea. She couldn't even move! She couldn't even get up and get herself something to eat! No wonder she never took care of me."

This was extremely difficult for Cecelia to accept, because she had believed all her life that her mother had deliberately withheld love and support. We took all the time we needed, though, and it wasn't long before Cecelia was willing to accept that her mother's lack of interest was not meant to deliberately hurt her.

"But what difference does it make anyway?" she asked. "It was still the same thing: she neglected me. She never held me. She hardly even touched me. I was a neglected child."

"I've got something for you to think about," I suggested. "And here it is: **All you have is NOW."**

"What do you mean?"

"I mean, yes, all that really happened to you and nothing can ever take it away, not really. Still, it happened *then.* You can remember it and we can work on it. In spite of everything, all you have is *right now*. In one sense, you don't even have tomorrow; you don't even have tonight. All you have is this one moment. When it's gone, you'll have the next moment. And in this moment, you can choose to do whatever you want. You can be resentful; you can be angry; you can hate your mother. Or you can do something different and be kind to someone or do a good painting or let go of an angry thought. You don't have to do this tomorrow or next week or forever, but you can do it right now, 'cause that's what you've got."

Cecelia said, "Oh, I get it! All I have is *right now* . . .."

I would like to say that Cecelia experienced one of those remarkable healings and never suffered after that, but it isn't true. However, I saw more and more improvement as time went by, and now, when I run into her, I can see a more positive, healthy, happy woman than previously.

It is a powerful concept: **All You Have is *Now***

Realizing that, you can undertake healing your past with much more confidence because after all, the past *is* in the past. However powerfully it affected you, the truth remains that all you really have is *this moment,* right now, to choose what you're going to do. That can free you to see things from another point of view, to choose to let go of immense anger and resentment, to try something else, something new, as Cecelia did.

Telling The Story New

James felt that people always took advantage of him. Whenever there was grunt work to be done, he always ended up doing it—cleaning up after a party, unplugging the drains, dejunking the car. Why didn't other people hold up their end of the work? How come it was always James that did the unpleasant tasks? He was sick of it, but he kept doing it.

He decided that he'd figure out when this all started, and right away he came up with an image of his family camping. He was the second of seven children, and his mother was constantly taking care of babies, cooking, cleaning, and responding to crises. His father, on the other hand, was a minister devoted not only to his congregation but also to writing theological commentary. While his mother tended children, his father sat in his portable director's chair writing and editing his extensive manuscripts. The rest of the children hardly did any of the routine camp work so it was left to James to gather wood, clean out the fire pit, carry out the garbage, and haul water, or so it seemed in his recollection. Whenever something wasn't done, James' dad would call out from his chair, "James! Take care of that fire pit *immediately!*"

One day, out camping with his fiancé, James realized he was not having a good time. In fact, he hated this whole trip. He found himself full of built-up fury just being at the campsite. So he sat down to think about it and then told Linda about it.

"I'd dislike that, too," Linda said. "You know what should have happened, of course. You should have hollered, 'Get up and do it yourself, you selfish creep!'"

"Yeah!" said James. "'Get up and do it yourself! What a selfish creep!" After a blaze of anger came a fit of laughing as James repeated, "You selfish creep!" several times over. His mind and body believed the new version of the story, and he and Linda enjoyed a great camping trip after that.

It's an odd thing. When we access a painful or infuriating memory, we can relive it in our mind's eye and then tell the story a new way. Sometimes it can be fierce and funny, like James' story, and sometimes it can be intense and poignant. If you retell the story with an emotional charge to the retelling, whether it's anger, humor or passion, something interesting happens. Your body and mind can begin to believe the new rendition of the story and voilá! You've got a new story in place along with a new emotional state associated with it.

As an example, when I grew up I had crooked front teeth. Whenever I'd ask my mom for braces, she would always say, "No braces. Look at Eleanor Roosevelt; she had crooked teeth and look where she ended up—rich and famous." The problem wasn't just my tender vanity; at school, the kids would call me Snaggletooth. That name burned itself into my being. Every time I looked in the mirror, all I could see were the teeth. Of course most of us feel ugly and unappealing when we're young, but I had no way of really understanding that. I just felt homely, a true Snaggletooth.

Later when I was in college, I found a way to put braces on my teeth and straighten out the problem, but I still carried with me the core belief that I could never be a pretty girl. My younger sister really was pretty (although oddly enough, she had front-tooth irregularities, too) and at a deep level, I just knew I could never be beautiful like her. This carried on throughout my life, a powerful belief that colored every relationship I had, every success I enjoyed, and most certainly, every failure. Whenever I'd look at photographs of myself, I burned with shame at how unattractive I was.

Much later, in fact not till my second marriage, I was able to resolve this. I was taking an online counseling course (www.theartoftheself.com) that taught remarkable concepts called "opening in" and "opening out." To put it briefly, you open your heart up (to yourself, in *opening in* and to others, in *opening out*) and see the person as the beautiful, whole, lovely child she once was. That way, you can accept her unconditionally and leave judgment and advice-giving behind, thus opening the door to true change.

I had no trouble with opening out; this was something I'd learned with my CranioSacral training and I felt I was quite good at it—accepting people unconditionally and caring deeply about them. However, it was a different case with opening in. Every time I thought about the little me, I was filled with a horrified sense of loathing and shame. The coursework suggested getting a picture of yourself as a little child to help with the process, but that only made things worse for me.

I was sharing ideas from the course one day and my husband entered into the process easily, opening out and murmuring kind words to the little me. How I hated it! I felt there could never be a pretty little Cathy. I told Russell how uncomfortable I was and he helped me figure out why. It turns out that I had been criticized a lot at home and ended up feeling that everything that went wrong was actually my fault (a very common pattern in kids). Russell suggested that I try to go back and see things the way they really might have been.

Doing that, I imagined my household of origin. There I saw an alcoholic dad and an overworked, overwrought mother. I saw children left on their own for hours at a time. I saw myself as an oldest child trying to bring some semblance of order to a disorderly and out-of-control home. For just a few moments, I actually looked into my own childhood face and saw—no kidding! —a beautiful child whose teeth were just fine after all.

At that moment, I decided to retell the story. "Little Cathy really was pretty," I said. "And her mom was there after school every day to give her a sandwich and milk and help her with her homework. Her brother and sister always were nice to her, too. She would brush her hair and look in the mirror and see how pretty she was." This was so sweet and affecting that I started to cry. I felt deep in my heart how wonderful that little girl really was. After I finished, things changed for me. I would sometimes look in the mirror and think what a gorgeous human being I was, and my family (and of course my husband) constantly reinforced that. It had taken a long time, but after that, I truly believed I was an attractive person.

Mental Dialogue

Sometimes therapists recommend that you write a letter to the person who harmed you so you can tell them exactly how you feel about what you went through. Sometimes you can mail the letter; sometimes you can't. I think this can be a positive method, but it has some drawbacks, because you never really leave the present moment. You never really forget you're the wounded adult who's trying to fix himself up. There's another way that works similarly but better. It's a conversation with the person who's not there. It works a lot like dialoguing with an affected organ or area in your body, only this time, you dialogue with the person you're concerned about.

As an example, Corinne was scared stiff of getting breast cancer. Every time she woke up, she'd obsess over it. Doing self-examinations, she was dead sure that she located some lumps, and her doctor indicated that there might indeed be some masses in her left breast. This sent Corinne into a terrible tailspin because her mom had died of cancer when she was a young teenager, and now she would follow the same agonizing path.

She came to see me and shared her dread about dying painfully as her mother had. She was pretty much convinced that she already had breast cancer, and at such a young age, too. Would her husband (with whom she was deeply in love) remarry? Who would take care of her little boys? And how could she possibly face the torment her mother went through?

We decided to think about her mom for a while. "Can you imagine her in your mind's eye?" I asked.

Corinne focused for a moment. "Sure," she said. "It's like she's right here. I can even feel her close to me."

"Okay," I said. "Why don't you ask her something?"

Corinne didn't hesitate. "Mom," she said. "I'm scared. I think I've got breast cancer and I don't want to die like you. What should I do?"

I didn't interrupt. In a moment, Corinne said, "My mom told me she wasn't really that scared when she got sick. She was actually pretty peaceful about it."

"Anything else?" I asked.

Corinne asked her mom again, "What should I do?" In a moment she said, "Mom's not convinced I'm really sick. She says I should go for a second opinion. She says I'm generally healthy and that I probably don't have breast cancer." A few more minutes of silence, then a break in her voice. "She says she really loves me and appreciates all I did for her. She says not to be so afraid. She says that if I ever did get sick, I would know just what to do." Corinne remained in a peaceful, relaxed state experiencing her mom's deep love for her. When we finished the session, she said she was going for a second opinion. She called me some months later about another issue and I asked how she was feeling about the breast cancer. "Oh, I'm not worried about that anymore," she said. "I don't have breast cancer and to be honest, I doubt I ever will."

This approach can be particularly helpful when dealing with past abuse. You can confront the perpetrator and tell him or her everything you're feeling. Combine that with Telling the Story New and you can clear out a lot of old pain.

As an example, a priest had sexually abused Jed when he was nine or ten. Jed's family was faithfully Catholic and had encouraged Jed to become an altar boy. Jed loved the beautiful cathedral and the elegant ceremony of Catholic worship; he loved being a part of it all. Unfortunately his parish priest had turned out to be a child molester. For Jed, the mingling of spiritual ceremony and sexual abuse had been horrible. Even today he could never attend a church without confusion and shame. He had undergone a good deal of psychotherapy but it hadn't taken him through it. One day, working with a gifted CranioSacral therapist, Jed once again addressed this difficult issue.

"Why don't you try talking it out with the priest?" suggested the therapist.

"No way!" said Jed. "I'll never talk to that guy again."

"No, you don't need to go see him. But if you want to imagine him being here, you could say whatever you like."

It took Jed just seconds to come up with a very lifelike image of the priest, so much so that he cowered from the sense of his presence, overpowered once again as he'd been as a child.

"Remember you're a grownup now," suggested the therapist. "You can talk to him from that powerful position. Let the grown-up Jed talk to the priest, not the child."

Jed did just that. He told that priest how wrong it was to seduce little defenseless boys. He pointed out the damage that it had caused him and every other child who'd been damaged by him. He brought up the harm it did him spiritually, cutting him off from church and God. Jed raked that priest over the coals. Afterwards Jed felt satisfied with a good job well done.

"So, are you finished, do you think?" asked the therapist.

"No, not exactly. What I'd really like to do is strap that monster to the railroad tracks and have a train run over him."

"OK, go ahead," suggested the therapist.

So in his mind's eye, Jed completely disposed of the sinful priest, and when he was done, he sat up and put on his shoes and socks. "That was great," he said. "I'm feeling free of all of that stuff. Ya gotta love it!" he said, reliving the moment when the train demolished the priest.

Forgiveness

Hearing this story, no doubt you're asking yourself, "How come Jed didn't just forgive the priest? It seems wrong to hold a grudge over all these years."

Many times, well-intentioned counselors and clergy urge people who have suffered at another's hands to forgive the perpetrators. People often answer, "How can I forgive him when he might do it again?" or "If I forgive him, he gets off the hook. But he really did those awful things."

I had to do a lot of thinking about forgiveness after my first marriage, which was abusive in many ways. If I forgave him, I would be excusing all the things he did wrong. I couldn't get past that injustice.

Finally I realized that when you forgive someone, it has nothing to do with *them* but everything to do with *you.* In other words, forgiving means that their misdeeds no longer bug you any more. There's no longer such an emotional charge to the wrongs they did. You can think about them as if they happened to someone else; you may feel bad about it all, but it's not overwhelming and it doesn't hold you back. To be honest, forgiveness may take years. I believe it should take just as long as it needs to take. If you force yourself to forgive too soon, it's like you're repeating the harm over and over again, only this time you're doing it to yourself. More important than forgiving right away is being willing to let it go when the time comes. In the meantime you can continue to work through the experiences and feelings, using StillPoint to guide you, till the moment when you're ready to do it in a healthy way.

Try It Yourself

The truth is, no one grew up unscathed. We've all got our share of pains and traumas to work through. Fortunately, we've got a whole lifetime to do it with; in fact, that can be the great adventure of our life, getting through and over the troubles we grew up with. With all my heart I believe that we can do it. I'm not saying that we will eventually end up with nothing bothering us; rather, I believe that we can continue to heal and grow into more and more happiness. You can use the some of these techniques yourself, coupled with StillPoint, to make it happen for you.

In Summary. . .

- You may be able to figure out where traumas originate by "counting back."
- Babies "remember" many things that happened to them.
- The body often knows what's wrong even when we don't thoroughly understand.
- Sometimes we need to scream or yell to let out some trauma, especially if we didn't cry or shout when we were traumatized.
- All we have is *now.*
- We can "dialogue" with someone who isn't even there in order to heal the past.
- Forgiveness sets *you* free but doesn't excuse the perpetrator.

Chapter Eight: StillPoint and Finding Your Future

When I came out of surgery, my husband was there waiting for me.

"They said it would be just an hour," he began gently. "But it was almost six. And I'm afraid there's some bad news. The lab says it's cancer."

Still wobbly from the anesthetic, I didn't know how to respond. This was my first surgery, a routine operation to remove a cyst under my right ear. How could I, the Herb Mama, have cancer?

The surgeon told us to make an appointment right away to start radiation treatment. In the days following at home, we considered that. If my life were in danger, it might be wise to at least consider the treatment, even though I wanted to find a natural cure.

One night Russell and I sat holding hands, thinking about the problem, and all of a sudden we were filled with peace, certainty, even joy. In that moment, we both knew that we shouldn't make the appointment—period. We didn't even think about radiation any more.

A couple of days later, the doctor called us at home.

"We sent another tissue sample up to University Hospital," he said. "It's not cancer after all; it's a tubular benign form of the tumor, very rare. I've never seen a misdiagnosis like this before. Sorry to have put you through that."

His call confirmed the clear knowledge that we received in StillPoint. If it really had been cancer, I have no doubt that we could have learned just the right approach to get better.

It's no wonder that individuals hire psychics or palm readers to discover their futures. How much easier it would be if we knew ahead of time everything that was going to happen to us! Indeed, alternative practices can entice you to find your future in lots of ways: divination, muscle testing, pendulums, reading Tarot cards or tea leaves, psychic readings of all types. I have no doubt that there are authentic practitioners among all these methods, but for me, there's always a bottom line: nothing works 100% of the time. I think that is one of the givens of being a mortal being on this earth: nobody can really foretell the future with 100% accuracy. I would say, however, that if you're willing to be patient as things unfold, StillPoint is a foolproof method of getting things right most of the time.

You just combine the principle mentioned in the preceding chapter; **All you have is right now,** with your ability to find StillPoint. In other words, in any particular moment, if there is the need, StillPoint can lead you to the correct decision that can shape your entire life or just make the present a little easier.

To understand how that works, we might remember how StillPoint operates generally. We live in a physical (or exterior) world, but there's a spiritual (or interior) reality to everything. Our spirits—or souls—or internal selves—or however you feel most comfortable in phrasing it—are connected up with the interior nature of the whole world. That connection makes it possible for our inner selves to know just about everything, if we're willing to take the steps to find out. Quantum physics makes this even more interesting because in that context, we're not even limited in space or time. Back to now and down to earth, our internal knowing is the way we can access the information we need to make the right decision, and StillPoint remains the easiest and most direct way to do it.

I particularly rely on StillPoint because, in contrast to some other methods, it brings you to peace and contentment rather than agitation. I also like it because you must find the answers *yourself* instead of relying on someone else. It's an odd aspect of our society, the fact that we're so willing to believe what other people have to tell us, even if it's about our personal lives. For me, I always measure any foretelling or intuition by this yardstick: Am I peaceful? Am I feeling sure? Does this lead to self-reliance?

You use StillPoint to make decisions the same way you use it for anything else. Take a breath, take a moment, and clear your mind and center yourself. When you feel that clear, calm moment of focus, think about the decision you need to make. Begin to run through all the possible options in your mind (I have also called this "scanning"). Rather than asking questions, phrase the possibilities as statements. When you hit upon the right one, you'll feel a deeper sense of peacefulness and rightness. That means you've probably hit on the right answer. You can repeat the process as many times as you'd like, just in case you want to feel more sure. Often when you hit on the best answer, you may think of various reasons *not* to do it that way, and it's perfectly fine to think through those reasons too. The final measure of correctness will always be peace, sureness, quiet certainty.

There may be times when you don't get any answer at all. I always take that to mean that it probably doesn't make any difference what you decide, one way or another. As an example, we live a couple of hours from one of the most beautiful national parks in the country, Arches National Park. The area surrounding the park is magnificent, and the adjacent town of Moab is just a lot of fun. Russell and I like to go down there to hike, wade in the river, and window shop. One evening, nearing the end of a long, hard school week, we discussed going to Moab for the weekend. We were looking for rest, renewal, refreshment. Neither of us had any particular feeling one way or the other—to go or not—so we decided to just leave it. Next morning, when it was time to go, we still didn't feel any inclination one way or the other. Evidently it didn't matter either way if we went, and perhaps this lack of an answer meant that we might go, but not get what we were looking for. We weren't ready to take one of those exhausting vacations that leave you more disjointed than when you left, so we decided to stay home and work on some projects instead.

However, it's just as true that momentary decisions may make all the difference in the world, when making the right choice, in *this* moment, can change the course of our lives. As a very sad example, Doris was the mother of a large family and the CEO of a successful boutique in a nearby town. At long last their family was going to take a vacation, a week-long break at a favorite lake resort. Doris and her husband Keith had prepared for many hours so they could leave their respective businesses (he was a tax accountant) in the hands of their assistants while they left. It was particularly hard for Doris to leave just then because her boutique was experiencing great growth and she wanted to ride the crest of the wave. It had been many months since their family had done anything together, though, and she felt the kids were fraying around the edges.

"Why don't you and the younger children take off earlier today?" she suggested. "I have just a few odds and ends to finish up for the bookkeeper, and I'll follow you with the big boys when I get done."

So in a flurry the family packed up and followed the plan. It turned out that Doris had just one more thing, and then one more, to finish before she was ready to close up shop. Satisfied that things were in order, at one in the morning she drove home, loaded the boys into the car, and pulled out into the night.

They drove for one hour, two, and Doris found herself getting sleepy. She didn't realize just how tired she was till she found herself jolting awake a couple of times. The third time, it was too late. She had fallen asleep taking a steep curve along a canyon road, and she couldn't correct in time. The car hit a shoulder and spun off the road, rolling into the canyon below. Although the two boys survived, Doris did not. That family lost their wife and mother in a moment when everyone was too rushed and frayed to get clear input on what to do.

Fortunately, most of our decisions don't include such life-wrenching consequences, but they might. Because this is true, along with my family I am trying to learn to "check in" every day when I have to make choices. Sometimes we get a clear indication of what to do; sometimes we don't. Still, it's always nice to know that you can get help when you need it.

When you're working with people in your career and especially when you're raising kids, StillPoint can be an invaluable resource in getting things right. Administrators (and parents) understand that there are too many variables to be able to decide by logic what to do. A lot of the time, you just have to rely on that gut feeling (reinforced by the peaceful confidence of StillPoint) to get it right.

As an example, Robert owned a small fast-food business located a few miles from his home. He had recently hired two managers, one day and one night, which freed him up to develop a store in another location. Robert left work one evening after inspecting the operation; all seemed well. Driving home, he centered himself and took a moment to see how he felt about the restaurant. "Everything's going okay," he said to himself as the first option. Nope, no peace on that. "Something's amiss down at the store." Yes, StillPoint.

Robert slowed, signaled, and turned around at the next light. He drove up to the restaurant just in time to see one of the waitresses storming out of the front door in tears. "What's going on?" he asked.

"You just ask that creep in your office," she fumed. "And don't worry. I'm never setting foot in this place again."

"Hey, hey, wait a minute," Robert said. "Tell me what's going on, and if there's something I need to do, I promise that I'll take care of it."

The waitress revealed that his night manager had been pilfering out of the till. When she confronted him, he turned around and accused *her* of stealing in front of the whole staff and several customers. Humiliated and furious, she'd stomped out of the restaurant just as Robert drove up.

"Do you have any proof of this?" Robert asked gently.

"You bet," she said. "Just check in his overcoat pocket if you don't believe me."

Robert entered his store and went back to his office, where the night manager was leaning comfortably at the desk having coffee. Seeing Robert, he jerked his feet quickly off the desk and sat upright. Before the employee could say a word, Robert slipped into the office and pulled up a chair.

"Do you have a moment?" he asked quietly.

"Sure, sure," the young man replied.

"Would you mind going over there and getting our coats?" Robert asked. "I have it in mind to go out for a bit."

"Uh, okay," said the manager, looking more and more worried. He gave Robert his coat, but Robert remained sitting. "Sit down for a moment," he said. "Would you mind going through your coat pockets for me?"

At first the employee made a move to walk out, but finally shrugged and sat down as he considered the alternatives. "OK, you've got me," he said, pulling a packet out of his pocket and placing it on the desk.

That placed Robert in a difficult position. The manager had not actually removed the cash from the premises, although he had clearly put it in his pocket. Robert sat quietly for a moment, clearing his mind and trying to figure out what to do next. He finally asked, "Is this all?"

That was the right answer. "Yes—well, no, I took some one other time," he said.

"How much?"

"It was last week. I took two hundred bucks. My car has broken down and I need to get it fixed. I was planning to pay you back, honest I was."

"Did you already spend it?" Robert asked.

"No, I needed this extra to get enough," the young man responded. "I'm really sorry, sir," he added.

Again Robert had to quiet his mind and try to find the best approach from here. He could call the police; he could demand witnesses; he could fire the young man and take the losses. Finally he felt peaceful about the following.

"I don't know if you've got a history as a thief or not. It didn't show up in your background check and I haven't been acquainted with you that long. The only thing I do know is that I left you in charge and you stole from me. And now we've got to decide what to do about it."

A silence—then the young man said, "Here, here's the money I was taking tonight. And I'll work for an extra week for free to pay you back what I took before."

"No go," said Robert. "But here's what you need to do. Write me a check for the two hundred you took last week."

"No, I can't do that!" the young man retorted. "I'm outa here!"

As he strode toward the door, Robert said, "OK, if you want to leave, there's nothing for it but to call the police. We've got several witnesses to your theft, and you admitted it to me, too."

The young man slowed and turned back. "If I do write you a check, what then?"

"Then you don't come back to work, you don't get your next paycheck, and you certainly don't get a letter of recommendation from me. But I won't press charges."

"All right, all right, I'll do it." The young man pulled out a checkbook and wrote Robert a check.

"You realize that if it doesn't clear, you'll be hearing from the authorities."

"I know it, sir. I'm truly sorry. This check will clear, I promise you that. I don't know what else to do about this." And he left.

After several days, the check bounced after all. True to his word, Robert went down to the police station and pressed charges against the night manager. He had felt in StillPoint that he should offer the young man a chance at redeeming himself, though the employee didn't take it. StillPoint allowed Robert to handle the crisis without falling apart as he offered the departed manager one last opportunity to regain his integrity.

Moms and dads need the assurance of StillPoint as much as employers do—even more, perhaps. Gloria tells this story: one day she was in the kitchen doing the dishes when the thought flashed into her mind to go upstairs and check the linen closet. She pushed the thought away—what could possibly go wrong with a linen closet? —and continued cleaning the kitchen. The thought recurred, a little more insistently and clearly: check the closet! So Gloria dried her hands, went upstairs and opened the closet door. There, placed by the pillowcases on the bottom shelf, was a burning candle. One of the children must have lit it in play and gone off while it was still burning. Paying attention to that mentioned saved her home. Of course, the kids got a firm lecture on fire safety as well.

When you're dealing with your children, StillPoint can save you when nothing else will. There are so many decisions to make every day with kids; some of them are meaningless and some of them may make the difference between life and death, between success and misery. There's no way a parent can figure it all out by herself, but StillPoint makes it a lot easier.

As an example, our daughter Miriam had been burning the candle at both ends the summer she was twelve. She'd gone to the water park, the amusement park, a girl's camp, multitudinous sleepovers and swimming parties, and more. She was just returning from a week at a friend's when *another* friend invited her to a big water park three hours away. In true Miriam style she was hell bent to go; nothing would stop her. She was visiting her friend when she called to get permission. I told her that she'd been gone long enough and needed to come home. Of course she wasn't willing to take no for the answer, so I told her we'd think about it and talk later. She called back a few minutes afterward and Russell took the call. As happens in most families, while Miriam wasn't willing to accept "no" from me, she did acknowledge it from her father.

When he hung up, Russ said, "I really don't mind if she goes. But when I checked to see if it was a good idea, instead of StillPoint, I got a brick," another way to say there was a block, not a flow. He checked a couple of times during the conversation and still got the same block.

As it turned out, Miriam came down with an earache and the flu the next day, spending the whole time in bed. Let me emphasize that there are not always obvious outcomes when you act on StillPoint, but there can be. And although this wasn't a life or death situation for Miriam, it was a good lesson: we can get clear answers on what we need to do any time we need them.

The time for such major decision-making came quite soon after that for Miriam. Like many junior high school kids, Miriam was always over-involving herself. She was elected student body secretary; she played basketball and soccer; she danced with the drill team. Pretty soon it seemed that she was gone more than she was home, and it was having its effect on her with frequent infections and occasional bouts of asthma, something new and uncommon in our generally healthy family. So we sat down with Miriam and had a talk.

"Something's got to go," we suggested. "You're going to be in ninth grade next year and you've got too many things going on. It's time to make a choice. We think sports are great and we also think you're a great dancer in drill team. But you probably ought to choose one or the other. It's kind of silly anyway," we smiled, "playing forward in a basketball game and then rushing to change so you can dance at half time."

She grinned at that. "But I don't know how to choose!" she sighed.

"Oh, we have complete confidence that you'll get it right," we said. "Just take some time and get back to us."

She took a moderate amount of time (for a young teen)—three or four hours. She tapped on our door and said, "I think I'm supposed to be in drill team," she said. "So I'm going to do that instead of sports."

"That sounds great," we said, "a good decision." Of course we would have said the same thing if she'd chosen sports, but the important thing was that she came to the conclusion herself.

As it turned out, Miriam really got a lot out of drill team. She worked hard on original choreography and ended up being selected as head captain of the team. Absorbed by fundraising, costume selection and creating choreography, she spent the rest of the summer happily busy with the team. And as it turned out, she made some lifetime friends with other kids on the drill team and with the advisors as well. We didn't use the term *StillPoint* with her; we just said, "Spend some time being very quiet and focus your mind on the question. Sooner or later, you'll have a peaceful feeling about the right choice."

We use this technique with our kids all the time. When our seventeen-year-old bumped heads with a serious scheduling problem at school (the schedule had placed student government—she was elected vice president—and Vocal Jazz, a coveted singing group she'd won a position in) during the same period. Maybe to us grownups that doesn't sound like a huge crisis, but it was the end of the world for Sarah in her senior year. The school couldn't budge on changing the schedule, so she had to make a choice. We told her the same thing: go through the options till you're peaceful. Fortunately she took enough time to come up with a new alternative: fulfill her student government position and sing with a college choir (which Russell directs). In that way she could do both things that she cared so much about. That brings us to another vital reality when dealing with challenges: once you back off from the strong feelings associated with a question or conflict, **there are rarely *only* two answers to your question.** By taking enough quiet time and really checking with StillPoint, you can usually come up with an alternative you might not have thought of before, something that can work out the best for everyone concerned.

Kids always go through this when choosing what college to go to. In most cases, eighteen-year-olds think they're ready to fly the coop and go to school somewhere far from home. Many parents want to keep their young people home for at least the first year, because many kids need another year or so to mature, and usually it's cheaper to do a year or two at a local college. Zane was in just this position. He wanted to leave home and go to State, but his mom and dad (especially his mom) wanted to keep him close. As often happens when kids are this age, the disagreement escalated until it was no longer a discussion but an argument. Finally Dad got a grip on the situation.

"Well, it looks like we've got different ideas about this," he said, "so let's just take some time off and think about it. We don't really have to decide for a while, even a couple of months if we need that long."

Zane wanted to launch into the argument again, but his dad put a hand on his shoulder. "I see your point of view entirely, son," he said. "We're not going to ignore what you want. But would you be willing to take a few days to mull this over? We'll do the same thing and get together on it later."

Zane and his parents had had enough experience with the principle of StillPoint that they were willing to keep in mind another important idea in decision making: **you usually don't have to decide right now.** So they agreed to think it over for a while. The parents discussed the issue together but left Zane to work it out on his own. Soon he came back with an option they hadn't considered.

"Do you have a minute to talk?" he asked his parents one night. That was a good sign; he wasn't in battle mode. They sat down together. "I can see your point about not going to State. It would be really expensive and my grades aren't good enough right now to get a scholarship. And I can see the good in going to a smaller college too. How about this? I could go over to Whitehouse," a small community college two hours away, "and live with Aunt Sue. I think I could help her around the house and make it worth her while to take me in. We could try that for a year and see how things go."

His parents thought this might be a good idea. They suggested that Zane call his aunt and see how she felt about it. Aunt Sue had just married off her last child and was going through empty nest syndrome. She would be all too glad to welcome Zane into her home. The family worked out all the financial considerations and Zane took off for school happy, leaving peaceful and happy parents as well.

Sometimes, however, you don't get a clear answer. Lisa, a talented horn player, was trying to figure out where to go to college. She had been offered scholarships at several good schools, and she just couldn't choose between them. She wanted to place herself in the perfect position to prepare to play professionally, which meant that she needed to make the right contacts. She thought endlessly about the question but could get no sense of direction. She counseled with her clergy, her parents, her teachers, and her school counselor; she even hired a psychic, but nobody could tell her what she needed to know.

Finally her band director sat her down. "You know, Lisa, sometimes you just have to make a decision," he said. "You're a fine musician. If you don't feel clear about what college to go to, just pick one. If it turns out to be less than ideal, no harm done. Sometimes it doesn't really matter what school we go to first off. So if you're not sure, then just take your best shot."

So Lisa let go of her angst and chose one of the scholarship offerings upstate. She played in the university symphony and in her junior year, auditioned for the city symphony as well, earning a position there. She played in both ensembles all during her senior year. During her last semester, she read an announcement about auditions for a large symphony in the state capital. "Hey, why not?" she said to herself. "It couldn't hurt to try." She scheduled an audition, played well for it, and was selected as a player. She graduated that spring and moved to the city, playing in the symphony and taking graduate classes at the state university. In Lisa's case, it really didn't matter that much where she did her undergraduate work. She took her best shot and did the best she could, and it worked out perfectly for her. The lesson of Lisa's story is that **sometimes it doesn't matter** what you choose. Not everything is an earth-shaking decision.

This goes hand in hand with another important reality about decision-making: you can have StillPoint about something but **it may not happen right away**. I recall those long years when I was a single mother with eight of my nine kids at home (along with all the friends and relations that tag along with teenagers). I was really only alone for four years, which seems like almost nothing from my perspective now. However, at the time, so far as I was concerned, I was going to be alone forever. In fact, my friends braced me for that obvious reality: a woman in her late forties with a passel of children at home had almost zero likelihood of hitching up with someone ever again. I tell the story of how it turned out differently in Chapter Two. Even though I *knew* in StillPoint that I could find my soul mate, it took a long time—more than two years—till we actually got together. During that time, it comes as no surprise that I seriously questioned the peaceful answer I seemed to be getting, but now, of course, it makes perfect sense.

Choosing whom you will partner with—who you'll marry, who you want to live with—can be one of the trickiest decisions, partly because of issues we discuss in Chapter Five. Often we fall in love with people who reflect our ongoing issues, not those that can be good for us. You can use the guidance in Chapter Five to help you decide on your partner. Remember, as I always tell me clients, **you have all the time you need** to make a decision. It's better to take your time and be sure, if you've got any doubts at all, than to rush into something and have to make expensive adjustments—both financially and emotionally—when it's too late.

The same suggestion works for choosing a career. Often we go into a line of work because our parents want us to do it, especially when we take over a family business. The pressures can be enormous. As an example, Carl's parents were working-class all their life; his dad was an auto parts salesman and his mother a caterer. They wanted Carl, their only child, to enjoy a better life than they'd had, and what could be better than going into law? Every lawyer had a nice house and luxury car. Carl was their dream child, intelligent and diligent. He would make a fine lawyer, and Carl's parents did everything they could to make that possible, including saving ahead for his college years.

A dutiful son, Carl graduated from college and then went to law school. He maintained good grades, but the truth of the matter was, he detested the law. He particularly hated having to take either side of an issue, when moral principles clearly declared one or another to be right. Not wishing to disappoint his parents, Carl went ahead and finished law school and passed the state bar. Then, at age 24, he had to do some serious thinking. It was time to look for a position in a law firm somewhere, but everything in Carl fought against that. It was a terrible conflict: satisfy his parents or do . . . what?

In his heart, Carl knew what he really wanted to do: work with troubled youth. In his law studies he had noted that effective intervention during the early stages of juvenile delinquency made all the difference for many kids in trouble. Unfortunately, if he took a position working with these kids, he would end up earning considerably less than his parents had hoped. Still, every time he thought about taking a position with a law firm, he felt like he was sinking into oblivion.

The moment of crisis came when he happened to see an announcement for just the position he wanted, the directorship of an alternative youth program in the city. To an outsider, the decision seemed obvious; Carl should do what he desired. Yet how he struggled with it! He knew his parents had sacrificed enormously to put him through law school and he was eaten up with guilt when he thought about going against their wishes. And yet here he was, with his dream ready to slip through his fingers. He came to his decision one night as he went through all the factors once again. When he thought about practicing law, he felt unhappy, agitated, confused. When he thought about applying for the youth center directorship, he felt total peace.

The next day he made his application and had the interview. It was a perfect fit. Within the week, he was offered the position and accepted it. He delayed telling his parents for some time, and when they finally found out, there were tears and plenty of recriminations for him. Nevertheless, Carl held to the course and kept his job. As the months and years passed, his parents began to see what an incredible gift he had working with troubled young people. The day finally came when they acknowledged to Carl that he had been wise in taking this job after all.

Just as important as one's vocation can be one's avocations—the stuff we do for love, for passion, for personal interest. There are so many things to choose from and it's so easy to become distracted, yet sometimes choosing a good avocation can turn into a tremendous benefit as time goes on.

As an example, Ruth felt like a frustrated artist. All her life she had been a social studies teacher, and a good one, but Ruth felt a nagging dissatisfaction with something in her life. She wanted to make stuff; she wanted to do stuff! She tried enrolling in the local tole painting class but that left her cold. She tried flower arranging—not really. Most days, after work, she just went home and noodled around the house, uneasy and frustrated. Clearly there was something she wanted to do but she couldn't figure out what.

As so often turns out, the chance to decide arrived quickly. Like many frustrated artists-in-embryo, Ruth loved to roam art supply stores. On a business trip with her husband, they took an afternoon to walk through an art discount house. Time and again she found herself drawn to the acrylics supplies. Her husband joined her there.

"Thinking about doing some painting?" he said.

"I, oh, I can't decide," she said.

"Tell you what," he suggested. "Why don't you just walk around the store and take a look at all the different media? When you come to the thing that attracts you the most, take a few minutes and see. Maybe that's the thing for you. I'll do the same thing!"

They did it. Ruth's husband ended up selecting some drafting supplies, since he had always been interested in building design. Ruth kept ending up at the acrylics counter.

"Looks like this is for you," her husband said.

"Oh, but I can't! It's so expensive! Look at all the different things," Ruth fussed, going into resistance as we so often do.

"Okay, let's look at it this way," her husband said gently. "You can spend maybe $200 getting set up for basic painting. Think about it. How much would you spend enrolling in a college course? Taking a weekend trip? Redecorating the bedroom? This is *important,* Ruth. Let's see what it would take to get started."

Before long, they had selected some basic supplies—paints, brushes, a book or two, art boards. They happened to pass by an adjustable art table. "Just the thing!" her husband said. Ruth started to protest at the cost, but got over her resistance a little more quickly. They walked out of the art store having spent much less than she feared, even for both their supplies.

As it turned out, Ruth had a natural aptitude for painting with acrylics. From the very beginning she turned out pieces that were original and interesting. Within the year, she had entered a local competition and had won second place. She continued with her interest, eventually teaching a community painting class. More importantly, her longing for something creative vanished. She'd found a true avocation, one that lasted her for years to come.

Of course, who knows? You may hit upon the right interest for now and later on find something new. Nothing is set in stone! However, StillPoint can guide you in the right direction for *now,* and you can enjoy satisfaction and more importantly, peace, when you follow it.

Instant StillPoint

Although in most cases, you will have plenty of time to make your decision, once in a while you will need to know *right now* what you should do. I want to emphasize that you don't always have to do long clearing and meditation to be able to access StillPoint.

As an example, a few days after Joe left a party early in order to avoid underage drinking (the story's in Chapter Five), he told us that the school principal had called him in for several interviews about the party. It had not been a school activity, but the principal wanted to nail a couple of the students, utilizing other kids to help her get the goods on the offenders. That afternoon, we got a call from the police asking about the party. We had to make a decision right then about what to do. We took a breath, centered quickly, accessed StillPoint, and then we knew.

"Thanks for calling, officer," we said. "But Joe did not stay at that party; he and his friends left the minute alcohol showed up. We do not feel it is appropriate for him to inform the authorities about those who were present at the event. It could place him at risk at some later time. It might be better for you to check with the parents for these details. Further, the school principal has been quizzing Joe and the other boys for the same information, including some harassment and threats. We feel that is inappropriate, so if you happen to meet with her again, we'd appreciate it if you'd tell her so."

The officer apologized for improperly involving Joe and his friends and promised to take up the matter with the principal. It would have been very easy to go weak in the knees when the police called, but StillPoint took us in a better direction. As it turned out, the principal stopped her inappropriate questioning and behaved more equitably toward the boys. The police eventually got their information through better sources. And Joe and his friends stayed safe in the school community.

You can use StillPoint in any pressing situation. You're lost—turn left or right? Someone at work is angry at you—defend your position or say nothing? Your car won't start—mechanical problem or out of gas? You've lost your wallet—look in the bedroom, the car, or call the police?

No doubt you're more organized than we are, because we're always misplacing our keys or wallet (more about that in Chapter Four). Most of the time we just look till we find it, and if we can calm ourselves down enough, we'll find it pretty quickly using StillPoint. However, one evening I was getting ready to go to the grocery store and couldn't find my wallet. We started looking for it and stopped.

"I don't think we're going to find it," I said, distraught.

"I think you're right," Russell said. "Where did you go today?"

We figured out that my last stop had been at the high school, picking up our daughter. Without a word, Russell and I got into the car and drove to the school. There was a basketball game going on, and he went in to check the Lost and Found. Before he even got to the office, there was an announcement on the loudspeaker. "We've just had a lady's wallet turned in," said the announcer. "If you've lost your wallet, please come to the grandstand office." He went right up to the office and claimed the wallet. Not a dollar or a credit card was missing. It's a great comfort in distress, StillPoint.

Try It

You never know whether the decision you face right now will be meaningless or can change your life forever. Most of us don't face the big choices—where to live, who to marry, what job to take—very often in our lives. But we do face multitudinous choices every day of our lives. You can use StillPoint to make those decisions work for you, short term or long. It won't be long till you're faced with one. Try using StillPoint to make the choice.

In Conclusion. . . .

- Your inner self, soul, or spirit (however you call it) is connected to the outer world.

- StillPoint can access the information you need to keep you happy and safe.
- If you don't feel any particular inclination when you're thinking through a problem in StillPoint, it's likely that the answer doesn't matter one way or the other.
- There are rarely only two answers to a question.
- Sometimes it takes a while for the results of your decision-making in StillPoint to become manifest.
- On the other hand, sometimes you can use StillPoint to make an instant decision when the pressure is on.

Chapter Nine: StillPoint and Healing the World

You may have heard the old Jewish legend of the Twelve Holy Men. The Talmud teaches that around the world are twelve holy men (I like to stretch the point and say twelve holy people, since who knows? Surely it's women, too) that hold the world together because they're naturally virtuous and upright. These people don't know who they are; they don't consider that they're particularly holy or pious; they don't even know each other. They could be gardeners, bankers, shoemakers, teachers, moms or dads. They could be rich; they could be poor. They might or might not belong to any religion. It doesn't matter, because each time they make a decision for virtue, they strengthen goodness in the earth. According to the legend, if any of them faltered and failed, it could signal the end of the world.

This story reminds us that even if we are unknown and unnamed, we can influence others—and maybe even hold up the pillars of the world—by the goodness we choose. That's what I call "healing the world." I believe strongly that our goodness *does* have a powerful effect on everything around us, and just as the flutter of a butterfly's wing is said to trigger a storm on the other side of the planet, so our kindness and goodhearted behavior can have widespread influence for good.

What does this have to do with StillPoint? Aside from the obvious ways that using StillPoint can enhance and heal us, I believe that finding StillPoint naturally increases our patience, kindness, generosity and compassion. The more often we deal with our problems by using StillPoint, the kinder our hearts can be, the more generous our souls. StillPoint calms us, helps us focus, and makes it easier for us to be better people.

You may remember the famous Mahatma Gandhi quotation: "*Be* the change you wish to see in the world." We can take this from the negative—when other people's behavior bothers us or annoys us, we can take the opportunity to observe those things in ourselves and eliminate them. We can also take this from the positive, that when we desire fairness, kindness and compassion, we can take each moment to become those attributes ourselves, moment by moment, incident by incident.

StillPoint is a wonderful asset in this endeavor, because in any circumstances, we can learn to center, calm, access our rhythm and find StillPoint on any particular issue. Every time you can on the challenge of finding StillPoint, it becomes easier and more natural, till finally you find yourself checking in and accessing what's best in any moment as a natural way of being. I like to think of this as a "bat life" because bats are always sending out and receiving radar messages so they can catch their bug dinners.

And, as we have mentioned before, using StillPoint naturally brings you into increasing compassion and gentleness, because what's truly good for you is going to be good for those around you. Beyond that, StillPoint just opens and softens your heart. You begin to understand what's really going on around you and can appreciate the sweetness as well as the pathos in people's lives.

For example, Evelyn was a teacher in a junior high school. Her daily schedule overflowed with too-full classes and noise; sometimes the demands of the aggressive kids erased the quiet needs of the subdued ones. Evelyn was tired and spent by the time she reached the end of most days, yet one Tuesday, she went home with something needling the edge of her mind. She couldn't figure out what it was, but after settling down with a cup of coffee in her quiet sitting room, she began to mentally list the possibilities. She was getting sick? She had forgotten to pay the bills? Was this something that had to do with her at all? No.

Something with the faculty, then, something political? No.

Something to do with a student? Yes, StillPoint.

Morning? No. Afternoon? Ah, yes.

It was second period English, she decided, and somebody in the second row over—ah, it was Dennis. StillPoint. She thought about this student. Normally he was compliant and productive in class, but thinking back over it, she realized that he seemed agitated and out of focus and had not turned any work in that day. Not only that, but he kept his head down most of the period. Evelyn thought some more. She could call his parents. . . .No. She could call someone tonight. . . .No. So she decided to wait till the next morning to find out what was wrong.

She kept a subtle eye on the students as they came in, and immediately noticed that Dennis was limping slightly and that his left eye was blackened. She knew that Dennis was not a fighter at school and indeed had few friends at all. After she got the students started on an assignment, she walked by his row and knelt down beside his desk. This small gesture of kindness was enough; the boy burst into tears, though he tried desperately to hide it from the other kids.

Evelyn said quietly, "Dennis, come with me." The other students wouldn't know anything more than the likelihood that Dennis was in trouble.

Out in the hall, Evelyn said, "I can see that something is bothering you. I'd like you to tell me, and maybe I can help."

Dennis did not speak for some time. Evelyn considered speaking again, but checked her rhythm. No, she felt, don't speak. Wait for him.

Finally the boy did speak. "I'm in trouble," he said. "But you can't tell my mom. He would beat her again if you did."

After a few moments of gentle discussion, Dennis revealed that his mother's boyfriend had been drinking a great deal and beating his mother. When Dennis tried to intervene, the boyfriend hit him, too, and knocked him down, thus the leg injury.

Evelyn listened for a few more moments, and then silently gestured for him to follow her. Together they walked to the counselor's office, and within moments, the counselor was on the phone to the police. That evening the boyfriend was picked up for assault, and the mother and son were safe at home. Further, the counselor helped the mother and son take steps to protect themselves from this abusive boyfriend, and within a few days, Dennis was back to normal.

Evelyn checked for StillPoint some days later to know if she should say something to Dennis. No—say nothing. So she remained positive and supportive to him—and the rest of the students, happy that she was a support in a difficult moment.

Sometimes our intervention will not even be that overt. One day, for example, my husband Russell was walking across the street to his building at the college. There at the crosswalk he observed a father and son. Dad was walking half a block ahead of the seven-year-old, who was carrying a backpack and struggling to keep up. Dad kept up a steady stream of commentary: "No wonder you're such a dork. Look how fat and slow you are. You're such a sissy. I despise that in a child. You should be more like me, not your mother." The child, a little plump indeed and tiring by the moment, kept struggling to keep up.

Russell's first response was to collar that gentleman and give him a quick, fierce lesson in parenting. However, he knew in the moment that that would only hurt the situation. So what should he do? The idea came to mind to stand and silently bless the boy, to send spiritual encouragement his way. "You're okay," he sent the boy this silent message, sending as much love and hope as he could through the power of StillPoint. "Be at peace. Don't worry about this. Things are going to get easier." He also asked God to send comfort to the child and to help the father recognize the harm he was causing. As the pair made their way along the sidewalk,

Russell felt that his silent spiritual support had at least calmed and encouraged that child—and that was all he could do.

Before we think that such intervention is useless, we need to recall that prayer, even impersonal, general prayer, has been scientifically shown to be efficacious. You may recall the study involving comparable wards in a hospital. Volunteers were asked to pray for the patients on one ward, while the other patients received no assigned prayers. The prayed-for patients experienced less pain, healed more quickly, and were released significantly sooner than the unsupported ones. The study repeated this process several times, and the results were always consistent. In other words, the good thoughts and prayers that we send others can make a literal difference in their lives. When we pray with the added stillness of StillPoint, the effect can be powerful for ourselves and for those we meet as well.

Jan, wishing to emulate Gandhi in being the change she wished to see in the world, had already been through real difficulties in her life. Jumped into a gang at fourteen, she fought her way out by the time she was seventeen, alive but much tougher. She got herself off drugs, stopped fighting, and regained control over her sexual life. By the time she enrolled in college at age 19, she was strong and street-wise. Therefore when she happened on a crowded fist-fight outside a college dance, she paused for a moment to assess. Should she go get security? No, no time. Should she scream? No, that wouldn't help. Call on that big guy in the corner to assist? No. It's up to me, she felt, and stillness descended on her soul. So she spread out her hands and moved in between the combatants.

"Stop fighting!" she commanded, all 5′3″ of her. The crowded hushed instantly and the two opponents stopped dead in their tracks.

"Now leave!" she ordered. She stood there emanating strength and assurance.

Within seconds, the crowd broke up and the two fighters took off in separate directions. The security officer monitoring the dance walked up to her.

"That was amazing," he said. "Thanks. How did you do that?"

"I've been in the situation before," she said briefly. Her personal strength, augmented by the assurance of StillPoint, was enough to defuse a dangerous, potentially lethal situation.

It doesn't matter what you do for a living; StillPoint can help you bring balance and peacefulness to your workplace and coworkers. Larry had a job booking reservations for a large airline in Los Angeles International Airport. Many of his coworkers felt frayed and worn out at the end of a stressful day on the job, but not Larry. Indeed, he seemed to emanate gentleness and understanding and hardly ever seemed tired. Often the porters would quietly direct short-tempered customers to Larry's line for his soothing touch.

One day, returning from a workshop many miles away, I got caught in a long procession of cars returning to the rental agency. By the time I finally got to the terminal, my flight had just taken off. I had attended with three colleagues, all women, all of us frustrated, exhausted and at the end of our tethers. We had tried two different reservation agents with the same result: sorry, next flight is tomorrow morning at 6:00 AM, sorry, you'll have to pay an additional $150 to change your ticket, sorry, sorry. At this time, we were all single mothers with no additional $150 to fork over, so we all slumped down on our suitcases and resigned ourselves to an uncomfortable night in airport terminal chairs. Just then I felt a tap on my shoulder. A porter gestured us over to the other side of the terminal. As we trundled our belongings over, a gentleman came around the side of the desk and took my bags out of my hands, carrying them gently to his station.

"How can I help you?" he asked quietly.

I told him our tale of woe, tears of exhaustion and defeat in my eyes.

"Ah, this is what I'm good at, problem cases. Don't worry, ladies. Let's see what we can do."

He didn't say a word more, but just punched away at his computer. "Oh yes, I see, the next flight is tomorrow at 6 AM." More typing. "OK, here's the flight change, no charge. Here's your hotel for the night, no charge, and here's your dinner *and* breakfast for the morning."

At this point I did burst into tears and took his hand, holding it for a moment. He squeezed my hand gently and said, "I know, I understand. I've got three kids at home myself. Just be sure now, ladies, to get yourself to the airport on time tomorrow morning."

I can't say if Larry understood anything about the mechanics of StillPoint, but his presence emanated peace and tranquility, the natural outcomes of StillPoint. Further, he seemed so fresh and quietly energetic, even under much daily pressure, that I'm sure he prayed or meditated in some way each day. I have no doubt he was one of those twelve Talmudic pillars at that moment.

This works well dealing with individuals and also when we deal with groups. For example, Sean had spent much of his life cultivating StillPoint through meditation and personal discipline. As a college freshman, he had dropped out of school and worked at manual labor for a number of years, during which time he found that he had a gift and passion for creating music. Sean met with the music chairman at the local college, got himself a composition scholarship, and settled himself into his life's dream, composing music.

Being out of school for a while had been both good and bad for Sean. He found that he had become a focused and passionate learner, but he also found that he needed to grow in classroom savvy, taking notes and doing papers and exams. Being a music major was especially hard because of the relentless pressure for high-quality performance.

Sean played viola in a chamber ensemble performing baroque and classical pieces. His performance skills were just fine, but he had a hard time meeting all the scheduled rehearsals and earning a living at the same time. Furthermore, the ensemble members were tense and antagonistic. When the pressure was on for a good performance, they turned on each other and snapped out their displeasure. This made for disagreeable rehearsals and potential disaster in performance.

So every time he attended rehearsal, before he packed up his viola to head for campus, Sean would spend a few moments finding StillPoint. He remained quiet as he descended more and more deeply into peace. Once there, he felt tremendous love and compassion for his fellow ensemble players, who were obviously reacting as they did because of extreme stress and pressure. Who knows what their troubles actually were, what their lives were like? Sean couldn't blame them for being touchy during rehearsal. Instead, he walked the few blocks to campus feeling quiet, mellow, loving. When he entered the rehearsal room a few moments late, heads flipped up in annoyance.

"I'm sorry I'm late," Sean said, smiling, emanating gentleness and peace.

Within moments, the atmosphere in the room changed. These musicians were sensitive enough to pick up the sweetness and stillness radiating from Sean, and they found themselves immediately more peaceful, quieter, happier than they'd been minutes before. The rehearsal went beautifully and during subsequent rehearsals, each ensemble member grew more and more kind and supportive to the others. By the time of the performance, these players had grown into an encouraging, cohesive group that delivered an inspired evening of music at the end of the semester.

Sean didn't actually have to *do* anything except bring himself into stillness and peacefulness. He brought these qualities with him into rehearsal. The same goes for you and me. Most of the time, it is impossible to know, intellectually, what would be right to heal any conflict or situation. However, if we emanate peace and compassion, that influence can often be enough to sweeten many situations and resolve conflict. If there had been some actual words to be spoken or actions to be taken, Sean would have known.

I had this kind of experience once while teaching in our detention center. One student, a tall, beautiful girl who had struggled through a life of abuse, neglect and drugs, seemed to be having a bad day. Nothing I said or did seemed to help; indeed, she got more and more angry and agitated as the hours went by. Finally she flew off the handle and yelled. "I'm not going to do anything for you, Mrs. Wilson. Forget it. F--- you!"

Since profanity was forbidden in our facility, I had to take action. Requesting that an aide remain with the class, I asked the student to leave the room with me for a conference with the facility staff, those who disciplined and cared for the students 24 hours a day.

We sat down together and I gathered myself. It was upsetting and a little embarrassing to have this girl blow up at me, but I took a moment to let it go and go into StillPoint. As we began our discussion, the staff member invited me to speak, but I asked the student to speak first.

And she did! She railed for ten or fifteen minutes about how mean I was, how I never gave her a chance to succeed, how I was always standing in her way, how she hated me.

Like most people, my first reaction was to defend myself against these accusations, especially because I always tried to be positive and encouraging to these kids. Should I answer? Nope, no StillPoint. Ask the staff person to intervene? No. What, what? I should ask her to speak more—StillPoint.

"What else?" I said. She stared at me, shocked. She was anticipating a fight, clearly, as most probably had happened in her life up till now.

"What?" she said.

"More, if you don't mind, please tell me more of what you're feeling."

To be honest, she was speechless for a beat or two, and then commenced on her harangue once more, but her heart wasn't in it. My request for more words, given in a spirit of kindness and compassion, took the sting out of her rant. She finished speaking and then I said, "My turn."

I just told her that I appreciated her work, that I was sorry if she felt unappreciated, that I wanted the very best for her, that I cared about her. That was all I felt I should say.

The staff member asked me what consequences I wanted to give her.

I was going to make a suggestion, but felt like I should stop. I turned to her. "What would you like to do about this?" I asked her.

"Uh, if I could have a few minutes to get myself together, I'll just come back to class, if that's all right," she said.

That was fine with all of us, and within five minutes, she was back in her seat, participating with class work as if nothing had happened. What *had* happened that morning? I wasn't sure, but I had the definite sense that whoever she was really mad at, it wasn't me. Since she was normally sweet and cooperative, I felt that I should let her get through her upset and join us, without repercussions. That's what we did, and everything went smoothly after that, till she was assigned to another placement by the juvenile judge. I was sorry to see her go. Dealing with her rage with StillPoint allowed me to get through—and out—of the situation with no hard feelings for me *or* for her.

In fact, teaching at the detention center taught me an important lesson: if I started the day in meditation and found StillPoint and peace, I could pretty much get the students and staff to see things my way throughout the day. You might think that detention center students would be unruly and difficult, and of course most of them come in that way. The program in our center is superb, though, at helping the kids move from resentment into cooperation. And beyond that, operating in peace throughout the day makes it possible to improve even the most obnoxious behaviors. The staff always says, "I don't know how Mrs. Wilson does it. With just a couple of words, she gets those kids to do anything she wants!" It's true. When I watch a classroom of these arrested kids belt out Christmas carols or write pages-long essays and stories, I know it's because my compassion and peacefulness have been part of creating an environment for success. It has been one of the great joys of my life.

If you turn out to be one of those twelve holy people who hold up the pillars of the world, maybe you will never know. But one thing for sure: learning and practicing StillPoint will bring you the compassion and kindness to truly make a change in the world and bring joy and goodness to everyone around you. Of course you'll be feeling better and better all the time too. As your Jewish grandmother might have said, "So what could be bad?" Give it a try.

In Conclusion. . .

- StillPoint can help us understand how to help people, either directly or indirectly.

Frequently Asked Questions

- What should I do if I can't seem to get to StillPoint?

Try doing some of the preparatory exercises without worrying about finally getting to StillPoint. Sometimes just being outside, or holding a sleeping baby, or digging in the garden—any of the exercises—can help you move toward StillPoint, and you may find yourself there without trying so hard.

- I live in the city and it's hard to get to outdoor settings.

Most cities—even big ones—make sure that there's good green space. Try to visit parks or arboretums once in a while. Even a garden shop or flower shop—or a well-appointed café or restaurant—can provide a dose of nature and help you with StillPoint.

- I am so busy! I don't have time for all these exercises.

It's possible to learn to find StillPoint without all the preparatory exercises. Try it out and see how it goes!

- I can't seem to get to StillPoint, no matter how I try.

Look in the phone book under massage therapy or bodywork, and see if there are any listed that mention Upledger or CranioSacral therapy. If not, make a few calls around to see if any practitioners have this type of training. Even just one session with such a therapist will get you going!

- Sometimes I think certain things are true in StillPoint, but then things work out another way.

The feelings and information we get in StillPoint aren't set in stone. It's not fortune-telling, and often we can't totally understand or interpret our impressions. StillPoint gives us a point of reference, a way of looking at things. It's a helpful tool but doesn't create an imperative.

- I want to be a therapist and help others with StillPoint.

Look up www.upledger.com or other schools that train in CranioSacral therapy. Classes are typically held in various locations and throughout the year.

About the Author

Cathy Wilson is a writer, teacher, and bodyworker. Over the years, she has published poetry and photography, taught drumming and dancing, and played in a recorder consort. At present, she teaches arts and writing in juvenile corrections. She and her husband Russell live on three acres in high-desert Utah.

www.ingramcontent.com/pod-product-compliance
Lightning Source LLC
LaVergne TN
LVHW090946080826
845145LV00003B/906